DAN HAWKINS

FINDING THE COURAGE
TO BECOME

OBSTACLES
PRESS

Second Edition, December 2018
10 9 8 7 6 5 4 3 2 1

Published by:

Obstaclés Press
200 Commonwealth Court
Cary, NC 27511

danhawkinsleadership.com

ISBN 978-0-578-43117-8

Cover design and layout by Norm Williams, nwa-inc.com

Printed in the United States of America

"*Swing* is jam packed with real life examples, success principles, and action steps you need to dust yourself off and get back up. No matter where you are in life today, Dan Hawkins lays out your plan to *Swing* for the fences. But it doesn't come easy. It takes that stuff in your gut that few have, but all want. It takes COURAGE. This book shows you how to get some. You won't regret this read!"
—Chris Swanson, M.P.A., EMT-P, AGO Spokesman

"The Revolution has arrived! Anyone who reads and applies what Dan Hawkins teaches in *Swing* is going to experience a lot more success in life. Some books are informational, while others are entertaining or fun. This book has all that, but it is also downright powerful! It's an instant classic. If you want a better life in the years ahead, *Swing* is one book you simply must read—and your kids, friends, and anyone else who wants to truly (and effectively) live their dreams."
—Oliver DeMille, *New York Times* Bestselling Author and Founder of Thomas Jefferson Education

Dan Hawkins has hit a home run in his new book, '*Swing*'! In my twenty plus years as an entrepreneur I have witnessed, by far, the biggest deterrent to success, failing to act because of self doubt and fear. Dan describes the most important ingredient to success, 'courage.' He inspires us through his own personal story. I have had a front row seat watching Dan's growth. I remember a shy young man who barely made eye contact when he first met me. I've watched him literally transform his life. In the book, *Swing* he shares the principles that he's applied. This book will inspire all of us to have the courage to become the person that God has created us to become.

—George Guzzardo, Life Founder

To my wife Lisa

who has always believed in me

and helped me discover

and live by the voice of courage

Be strong and courageous...

—Joshua 1:9

CONTENTS

PART TWO: COURAGE IN ACTION

FOREWORD

Dan Hawkins is a modern day David over Goliath success story. Without funding, connections, or any previous entrepreneurial experiences, and despite dealing with massive fears that practically paralyzed him, Dan and his lovely wife Lisa did what others said was impossible, namely, escaping the *Financial Matrix* and living their dreams with their five daughters—without 9-5 jobs. Dan and Lisa applied the financial principles that are taught in the *Financial Fitness Program* to turn their visions into reality and today live on a picturesque property with a custom-built mansion, attached horse-farm, and numerous recreational vehicles. How many former mechanics (Dan) and day-care providers (Lisa) live like this? The material blessings, however, are merely the frosting on the success cake. In reality, the real value of the dream is who one becomes on the journey to success. Learning how to do this is the purpose of *Swing*.

Indeed, I know of no one who has overcome more fears to achieve his dreams than Dan Hawkins. Whereas Dan's limiting beliefs held him hostage to past failures, buried within this seemingly quiet, shy, and introverted mechanic was a fire that continued to burn. This fire eventually burned away his fears and revealed the champion within. To be sure, at the beginning Dan failed repeatedly in his efforts to conquer his Goliath-like struggles, but when a man knows why he is doing something he can endure almost anything.

Dan, similar to David of old, knew Goliath must fall in order for him to fulfill his destiny. Thus, he simply grabbed another stone, faced his nemesis and fought until the giant fell. Dan is living proof that actions conquer fears, actions that anyone can do, but sadly few follow through. Dan realized that dreams are a more powerful emotion than fear, and that when dreams are fed to the subconscious mind more than fears, the fears will fall. This is the story of Dan Hawkins, a story of dreams, struggles, and ultimately victory, all because a man refused to let his fears steal his dream.

In the following chapters, the reader will learn how to overcome fears and roadblocks by enabling the courage within. However, beyond mere information, this book provides the inspiration to act! It is said that knowledge is power, but in reality, only knowledge applied is power. The reason Dan's story is so inspiring is that he used his dreams as inspiration to apply the information he learned. Moreover, he didn't just stop at his own success; he also shared the powerful principles in this book to bless others who are seeking their own success in life.

Above all, this book displays courage because, rather than strike perfect poses of success for the readers, he instead reveals his biggest challenges and fears. Dan, in short, cares more about the reader's success than his reputation. After all, truly successful people seek to make a difference in others, not a name for themselves.

This, in my opinion, is what makes this book special, for Dan reveals how a person can overcome improper programming through purposeful dreams, powerful courage, and passionate actions. His life models the book's keys to courage (believing, dreaming, listening, and acting) until victory is assured. Dan and Lisa are not only life-long friends and business partners, but also people who inspire my wife Laurie and I to continue growing. I want to personally thank Dan for leading with character, courage, and conviction. His light shines into the darkness and has helped thousands of others see more clearly the path to financial freedom.

—Orrin Woodward, *Inc. Magazine* Top 20 Leader, Top 100 Speaker, and *New York Times* Bestselling Author

THE COURAGE TO BEGIN

*"Courage is not simply one of the virtues,
but the form of every virtue
at the testing point."*
—C.S Lewis

I was twelve years old, and the tears wouldn't stop. Yes, it was a hot summer day. In fact, it was one of those youthful summers that seemed to last forever. But the heat didn't cause the tears. The truth is that most of my time that year, and several other years, was spent trying to fit in—and learning more than I really wanted to know about social awkwardness. I have more experiences with that struggle than I would like to remember, but one event stands out in my mind like it was yesterday.

Here's the good news: My baseball team and I had worked our way to the championship game. I had been a part of this team since the second grade, and being on the verge of achieving our highest goals was incredibly exciting. Most of the time I was able to just blend in and avoid being noticed, which suited me just fine. I wasn't the worst player, and I certainly wasn't the best. I moved around from pitcher to first baseman, and to center field. I was always a starter, but never a star.

NEXT BATTER!

Then it happened. It was late in the game, we were down, and the bases were loaded. It was my turn at bat. As I put down the extra bats I had been using to warm up, I was filled with overwhelming fear. I was terrified, in fact. At the time I was too scared to focus on why I was feeling so much fear, but

> **I was afraid to fail, afraid to look bad in front of everyone, and afraid to let my team down.**

looking back now I remember: I was afraid to fail, afraid to look bad in front of everyone, and afraid to let my team down. Most of all, I was scared to ultimately prove what I had been telling myself was true, that I was a failure. I knew I would fail. I just knew it.

I walked up to the plate and felt tears began to form in my eyes. My legs began to shake. In my head I had already lost. It was just a formality now. The first pitch sang through the air and snap—the ball hit the catcher's mitt. "STRIKE" yelled the umpire. I didn't even bother to move my bat off my shoulder when the pitch came. I was now one-third of the way to my predicted outcome.

The tears began to stream down my face, cutting lines through the dust my skin had collected on this hot, dry summer day. As I stepped away and looked down the third base line, my coach gave me the best encouragement he could and flashed me the sign to *Swing*. Stepping back into the batter's box was not easy. More tears clouded my vision, the shaking in my legs escalated, and I felt so weak and numb that I could hardly muster the strength to move.

The next pitch seemed to come in slow motion. It was right there for the taking—the size of a volleyball, it seemed. But it felt like my arms weighed a thousand pounds and I couldn't **Swing** the bat. "STRIKE TWO!!!!" the Umpire's voice told everyone of my failure. I remembered what my coaches had repeated so many times: "If you don't *swing*, you can't hit the ball. Don't just stand and watch it go by. At least try to hit it." I tried to swallow, but my mouth was too dry. "Why didn't I *swing*?"

It was all but over now, I knew. I wiped the tears from my eyes and looked over at my teammate warming up on deck. Nate, the star player, had no fear. I knew he was filled with unending courage and confidence. But me? I looked back at the pitcher.

THE INNER BATTLE

"The bases are full," my mind was racing, "and any hit could drive home the winning runs." The thought quickly passed through my mind: "What if I were the hero? What if I could gather the courage to just *swing*?" I knew it would take so little effort on my part. All I had to do was *swing*, like I had thousands of times in practice. "Do I have what it takes to win? Is there a champion in me waiting to get out?"

Just as fast as these thoughts came they were replaced with an old, familiar voice: "Dan, who do you think you are? You never win. Don't try, you may fail. Leave the bat on your shoulder, at least you can always look back and say you didn't even really try. Better than trying and failing." I wondered for a second if I would actually *swing* this time (I wanted to), but I never really believed it.

The sound of the ball snapping into the catcher's glove, the yell of the umpire "STRIKE THREE, YOU'RE OUT," and still the bat resting on my shoulder. *Yet again, the courage to act eludes me, but then again what could I expect, this is just who I am.*

As I walked back toward the dugout, crying and ashamed, the story was written. *Dan is good enough to play, but lacks the courage to be a champion.* Nate stepped up to the plate, the pitcher sent a fastball down the middle. The crack of the bat seemed to seal in all of my thoughts. Not only did Nate drive in the winning run, he hit a grand slam and saved the day.

I participated in the celebration of our victory, but during the outward cheers and storming the field my inner voice kept telling me: "Maybe only a few people have what it takes to hit a home run in life, and maybe I'm not one of those people." My chest was tight, and the smile on my face tried to hide what I was really feeling. *Something is really wrong with me. I'm just not good enough to succeed…*

CONVINCING OURSELVES

It seems that from that day forward, this was the story that played out—over and over—in my mind. In high school, at college, dating (or lack thereof), getting a job and starting a business, and in every walk of my life, this plotline seemed to color everything I did. It was the same old storyline, repeated again and again. I became a car mechanic largely to avoid having to deal with people, and I made so many other choices for the same reason. I kept hoping I could just remain hidden away, not required to stand up and be seen as a failure. Opportunity to *swing* came up so many times, and…the bat stayed on my shoulder.

Tears, fears, failure—and watching someone else respond to the same opportunities and win the day. "Something needs to change," I told myself, every time I failed to take courage and take action. Then…I…didn't do it. "That's who I am," I convinced myself. I did this so often and so strongly that I really thought I had became that person—all the way through. Inside and out.

Until I changed…

THE ROAD NOT TAKEN

And the change came in a huge way. In fact, it came through the Naaman Principle, the idea that truly successful people do a few simple things, and do them consistently—little, vitally important things that make all the difference. Unsuccessful people simply don't do these things. More on that later. But once I changed, I realized that the courage to *swing* the bat had been there all along. I just didn't have the tools…or so I thought. But learning these tools changed me in a powerful and exciting way.

Now, many years later as a millionaire, author, and successful business speaker, I meet men and women around the world who have spent most of their lives with the bat on their shoulder. Afraid to *swing*, afraid to take a chance to become everything God created them to become. So many people have given up and put a period in their life where there should have been a comma. Or, better still, the chance for an exclamation point!

I write this book, not because I am proud of my accomplishments—even though I am, and even though I'm very grateful to those who helped me see what it takes to simply take courage and take action. I write because I was given a chance to change, and in the process I learned how to lift the bat and *swing*! I was given the encouragement and mentoring to grow, and I want, with all of my heart, to help you take your swings too.

All of them.

Most of us are tempted at some point in our life to fall into a recurring trap of shrinking, avoiding, failing to step up and really go for what we truly want. Many of us stay stuck in this way of thinking and acting for years or decades. Or always. It was not until I was in my mid-twenties that I was given the tools to break this cycle. It took surrounding myself with great people and great ideas to realize that anyone can rise above his past, his fear, his inner voice of self-criticism and self-doubt, and win in life.

> **Most of us are tempted at some point in our life to fall into a recurring trap of shrinking, avoiding, failing to step up and really go for what we truly want. Many of us stay stuck in this way of thinking and acting for years or decades.**

The truth is we already have the courage in us to make such changes, but some of us need a little help to bring it out. We were all created for a purpose. The question is, will you develop the courage to find and live yours?

STAND AND DELIVER

My life is a story of struggle and change, fear and faith. Whenever I consider the many experiences of my life I see signs of courage and also lack of courage. Which brings up a question: Why did I have courage in some moments and not in others? I believe courage is within all of us, we just need to learn to embrace it and cultivate it.

In this book I will share stories of courage and fear (and they often go together). Too many times in life I sat with the bat on my shoulder, afraid to *swing*. Too often I let fear run my life. Learning how to develop courage has changed every aspect of who I am, and it has impacted all areas of my life. I will share stories, some very personal, about how courage or lack thereof determined the outcome of so many events. Learning to muster the courage and push past fear proved to be the key in my marriage, parenting, finances, faith, and business success.

> **Wherever you are right now in your life, fear is the thing holding you back. Some fear stands between you and whatever you really want in the years ahead.**

The same is true for everyone, I believe. If we keep the bat on our shoulder, we are letting fear determine how we live. The courage to *swing* is essential if we want to succeed, in anything, ever. But this is easier said than done. Wherever you are right now in your life, fear is the thing holding you back. Some fear stands between you and whatever you really want in the years ahead.

THE COURAGE TO ACT

Knowing how to push past your fear and do what will bring you what you want—this is a powerful lesson and skill. Those who learn how to do it, and use this understanding, are able to consistently progress. Those who don't, too frequently find themselves in a rut, wanting more, but standing here on this earth with a bat on their shoulder while the pitches of life fly by. One after another.

This book is about becoming the kind of person who changes this pattern and swings. In short, real success in life doesn't come to those who stand there with the bat on their shoulder. To live the kind of life we really want, we need to *swing*! Most importantly, this book is about how *you* can become such a person.

I did. You can.

One thing I know, and all successful people know it as well, is that whoever you are, there is a fear (or fears) standing between you and what you really want. This is just the way life is. But fear isn't nearly as powerful as it seems. Not when you have a bat in your hands.

So get ready. Because we're going to learn how to lift that bat and really use it in your life. It's time to *swing*! And I can attest from personal experience that this one important change will make all the difference.

"BATTER UP!"

PART 1

THE VOICE OF COURAGE

*"It's supposed to be hard. If it wasn't hard, everyone
would do it. The hard...is what makes it great."*
—A League of Their Own

*"I'm thirty-six years old, I love my family, I love baseball,
and I'm about to become a farmer. And until I heard the
Voice, I'd never done a crazy thing in my whole life."*
—Field of Dreams

CHAPTER 1

THE COURAGE TO BELIEVE IN YOURSELF

"You will never do anything in this world
without courage. It is the greatest quality of the
mind next to honor."
—Aristotle

In the study of success and the life of any successful person, you will always find a story of courage. Many times it is a quiet courage of someone who just won't give in, sometimes it is a child with a bad past overcoming a label, and other times it is a story of life or death on a battlefield. The story of great courage recurs in all tales of success, because it is a necessary part of achieving anything important.

PRINCIPLE 1

INITIATE

TAKING COURAGE IS THE FOUNDATION OF ANY AND ALL SUCCESS.

(Without courage, there is no success. Any success is found on the other side of courage. In other words, between you and what you really want stands fear. Overcoming it isn't one way to find success in your life— it's the *only* way.)

This applies to marriage, family, business, sports, leadership, art and science, the military, and every other field of human endeavor. Stories of courage inspire us, give us hope, and make for great movies, but can we all tap into this type of courage in our everyday lives?

Let's start by defining courage. According to Wikipedia: "*Courage is the ability and willingness to confront fear, pain, danger, uncertainty, or intimidation. Physical courage is courage in the face of physical pain, hardship, death, or threat of death, while moral courage is the ability to act rightly in the face of popular opposition, shame, scandal or discouragement.*"

Success in anything demands pushing past your current comfort zone and becoming more. When I first became an entrepreneur, everything I needed to do to become a success scared me. My biggest fear was the fear of people, or more to the point, what people thought of me. One night as I was struggling to push past my fear, I had an argument with myself, and this question kept repeating in my head: Do I have what it takes to be a success in business?

Because I had a history of filling my head with examples of failing to have courage, this was a dangerous question. You see, the business I wanted to build focused on working with and leading people. The fear kept coming—when I tried to go to sleep at night, during the night, when I first woke up in the morning, numerous times during the day. Every thought of building my business brought waves of worry and fear.

AS A MAN THINKETH

To this point in my life, no one would have picked me as someone likely to build a people or leadership business. I certainly wouldn't have. But here I was, trying to figure out how to get past my fears and go for something I really wanted.

It was during these tough, relentless, internal dialogues with myself that I experienced my first breakthrough. Call it a seed of courage, or maybe the foundation of courage. At first, the two inner voices in my head debating whether or not to overcome my fear and build my business, or simply give up and stop fighting for it, were equally matched. In fact, they leaned more toward giving up than mustering my courage.

But the battle continued. I kept telling myself that I wanted this, that it was time for me to make a change, and that I could do it. I didn't fully believe any of this, but part of me did. And instead of giving up right away, I keep engaging this internal discussion. Should I do it, or should I quit?

Somehow, I kept telling myself that this was something I needed to do. I just kept arguing with my doubts and fears. This wasn't courage, not by a long shot. But it was something just as important. It was a seed of courage. A grain of courage. A start.

> **Just like the Bible teaches that the faith of a tiny little mustard seed can bring about great miracles, a little seed of courage is the foundation for even more courage. And guess who has such a seed of courage? Answer: Everyone.**

Just like the Bible teaches that the faith of a tiny little mustard seed can bring about great miracles, a little seed of courage is a foundation for even more courage. And guess who has such a seed of courage? Answer: Everyone.

This is true. Everyone has that seed of courage inside. It's just part of being human. And it is very real.

This is the great thing about overcoming our fears. We already have the seed inside. We just have to nurture it, and allow it to grow. Like any seed, when it grows, it becomes so much more than the tiny little thing it is right now. That's the first thing you need to know about overcoming your fears and having the courage to become: It's already inside you. The seed is there.

If you're like me, you may have never quite given the seed enough water or sunlight. You might have buried it deep, too deep to sprout. You may have convinced yourself over and over, in a thousand thoughts and choices, that you just aren't a person of courage and success. But the seed is still there, just waiting for a chance to grow.

PRINCIPLE 2

DREAM

THE SEED OF COURAGE IS IN YOU. LOOK FOR IT. FIND IT. FOLLOW YOUR DREAMS.

(Always. This is true of everyone. Nobody is an exception to this rule.)

FOUNDATION OF COURAGE

Success requires a foundation, and that foundation is courage. Without courage, we simply won't do what it takes to succeed in life, or in anything—big or small. Moreover, the foundation of courage is a *seed of courage* that is already inside you.

Where does this foundation come from? Looking back now, with the benefit of understanding courage and what to look for, it is clear that it grew and took shape in me for many years. The early part of my life was marked by a lot of moving from small town to small town. The move that stands out for me the most occurred when my family relocated to a small farming town in northern Wisconsin. I was 7 years old.

My dad always had a dream to run a dairy farm, like most of his family, and he finally got his chance. Now, when I say small town, I mean *small*. The community was named Ogema, and it had about 300 people. Any "real" store was a good 30-45 minutes away, depending on the weather. It was your typical small midwestern town, with a church, gas station, small country store, three bars, and a lot more fireflies than people. The light of the fireflies was magical during summer nights. For a kid, living on the farm was not a bad deal. We had land to explore, ATVs and horses to ride, and lots of chores and activities.

I learned a number of important foundational lessons while I worked on the farm. One of the most important lessons was the value of money. For example, I was given a calf every year that I could sell for cash or raise for a bit and sell for a bigger return. That was my pay for helping out on the farm.

The first time I got paid I raced to the small store and loaded up on candy, then I enthusiastically ate most of it in one afternoon. I quickly found myself broke and suffering with a memorable stomachache. After that I started to save a little. I learned how to protect my investment and care for my calf so I would get a better return.

I learned a lot from the behavior of the people around me, such as my dad's hard work and how encouraging my mother was on many occasions. Also, my sister provided a good example of courage. One time, for example, she was missing and we looked everywhere trying to find her. We finally heard a faint voice, and found that she had climbed to the top of the silo. If you've ever seen a grain silo in person, you know what a big deal this is! I remember thinking: "She isn't afraid of anything."

I also learned that hard work is key to a good life. I watched my dad get up early and stay out late most days just to keep the farm going. I did not realize it at the time, but to pack up your family and move to a small farming town and try to make it as a farmer took a lot of courage. My dad had a dream and he took his shot.

The next couple of years were tough; my parents grew apart, finances were a struggle, and ultimately my dad had to give up on his dream and move back to the city and a 9-5 job. A lot changed at that point. My dad lost the spark in his eyes, he became more disengaged with us and just began to live a work-and-sleep life.

I learned that the spark in one's life is really important. Take the passion away, and you lose so much of yourself. There was a brief moment where I saw the spark return. My dad was a very talented artist, but I didn't even know about his talent until a dream inspired him one day. He was told about an opportunity to get a job where he could start apprenticing with a company and learn to be an architect. I watched my dad come alive again and begin to draw things around the house almost every day for about two weeks. It was like living with another person—like the early days on the farm again.

As I said, I had no idea he had this talent, but the dream gave him the courage to bring it out, dust it off, and put it to use. For reasons I still don't know, this opportunity didn't work out. This sent my dad back into the disengaged life. For many years my father kept "the bat on his shoulder", so to speak, and gave up on his dreams. This led to a lot of pain, including the divorce of my parents.

I powerlessly watched my dad return to spending all his time making a living while forgetting to live his life. The dreams were gone and he began to live the quote by Henry David Thoreau: "Most men lead lives of quiet desperation and go to the grave with the song still in them."

> The dreams were gone and he began to live the quote by Henry David Thoreau: "Most men lead lives of quiet desperation and go to the grave with the song still in them.

Looking back at all this, I realized that as a boy I learned a lot about chasing your dreams. For example:

- It takes everything you have to muster the courage to pursue what you really want in life.
- Sometimes things do not turn out the way you hoped they would, but it is essential not to lose your spark.
- Life can be very hard for everyone, including those who are pursuing their dreams and those who aren't, but those who do keep seeking their dreams seem a lot happier most of the time.
- Chasing and achieving your dreams is challenging—and few people push past their fears and do it in spite of whatever difficulties arise—which is why only some people really succeed.
- You are the happiest when you pursue the dreams God has placed within you.

> **You are the happiest when you pursue the dreams God has placed within you.**

Even though I can say I learned these lessons, largely by watching my parents and other people in my life, my early choices show that I didn't truly understand what I was learning. Indeed, it is almost as though I used my dad's example to justify not chasing my own dreams. *That's just who I am,* the old voice told me too many times to count.

THE POWER OF YOUR DREAM

As a young adult I decided to become an auto mechanic, not because I had always dreamed of working on cars, but simply because my stepfather owned a small dealership and I just naturally ended up working for him. It was much easier to get a job with my step dad than to venture out into the unknown and pursue something else. And I liked the solitude of the work: the beautiful thing about working on cars is they don't talk back, or expect you to talk with them.

Actually, my dream at the time was to become an automotive engineer. However, the more I learned about this career field, the more frustrated I became. To become an engineer meant leaving the security of my hometown and going off to college. I asked myself repeatedly, *how can I ever become a successful engineer if I lack the courage to leave home for college?* I couldn't come up with a satisfying answer.

This led to one of the more embarrassing periods of my life. I eventually choose to forego engineering school and attend a local tech college and become an automotive technician. It was a major letdown from what I really wanted, but I let my fear choose my path.

This decision meant I could still live at home and work for my family business, remaining firmly within my comfort zone. But the most embarrassing thing came later. The truth is that at this point in my life, after the baseball experience, I was used to avoiding hard things if I could, and I constantly reminded myself that courage was something I just did not have.

In fact, my difficulty in working with people made the simplest phone calls very difficult, if not impossible, for me. Even at age 18 I asked my mom to make all of my haircut appointments because I was afraid to talk to people. To make matters worse, getting my haircut was painful because the hairdresser always wanted to talk.

Not only was I afraid to make the phone call, I dreaded the whole process. I dreaded people. It was a serious problem. In fact, it was not until age 23 that my mom stopped making my appointments, but this only changed because I got married and now my wife did it for me.

I chose the local tech college to avoid taking any scary risks, but even this had its share of challenges for somebody as afraid of new things as I was. The first step was orientation for my freshman year. This is where it gets really embarrassing. I was so nervous to attend, I kept struggling with self-doubts, and I battled with constant thoughts about just dropping out. I tried every way possible to justify not going to college and still succeeding as a technician.

I suffered all of this fear and worry not just because I didn't want to go to college, but also because I did not want to *start* college. Knowing I couldn't quit once I started, and that my future was resting on this degree, I did what no 18-year-old young man would do, ever. I asked my mom to come with me to the orientation.

I should say right now that I don't really love sharing these embarrassing stories about myself. But I want you to know that if I could get past my fears and become a successful businessman and speaker, anyone can. You can. I know, because I did it. I lived this. The orientation should have been a turning point for me, just like the championship baseball game. I should have swung at those pitches, and I should have mustered my best courage and gone to the orientation alone. But I did neither of these things. I let fear take the lead, and let Mom take the seat next to me.

EYES OPEN

The idea of taking my mother with me to the orientation, as you can imagine, seemed like a good idea right up until the moment we walked into the room full of men. We were in the meeting no more than 10 minutes before the head instructor looked at my mom and asked, "Who are you? You aren't on my list." To which she replied: "I'm Dan's mom." My face instantly turned bright red. I began to sweat, and wished I could just vanish into thin air. This was one of the most uncomfortable situations I have ever experienced.

It was at this point that I learned something unexpected. Something surprising. I wish I would have found an easier way to learn it, but the hard way certainly did the trick. In short, while I sat in that room with the other men and my mom, I realized that the thing I had feared (going into a new situation with people I didn't know) was a lot less embarrassing than what actually happened because I lacked courage. What possibly could have occurred at orientation that would have caused me more humiliation than everybody realizing I needed my mommy!

This was a repeating pattern, I realized. Every time courage was required and I did not display it, my lack of courage was reinforced—and things got worse. My cowardice was actually more costly than courage would have been.

As I look back on my life, it is so clear that this lack of courage—and letting fear guide my choices—was the main component in every area of struggle. I should have learned this lesson that day on the baseball diamond. Acting out of fear (or not taking action for the same reason) brings worse results than whatever you're scared of. It really does. Fear is the enemy, every bit as much or even more than the thing you're trying to avoid.

During the baseball game, I didn't even *swing* the bat. I didn't try to hit the ball. I let my fear of failure *absolutely ensure* that I failed. Somehow I didn't quite grasp this lesson until later. At the time of my college orientation, I still hadn't learned to at least "*swing* the bat," to at least try. And taking "mommy" to college with me was even worse than not swinging at the pitches in the championship.

> **Giving in to fear often brings worse results than whatever you're trying to avoid.**

CASEY'S WAY

This lesson is essential. But it's not always easy to learn—at least it wasn't easy for me. I've learned over the years that a lot of people face the same struggle. It's hard sometimes to remember that giving in to fear often brings worse results than whatever you're trying to avoid. It reminds me of the great baseball poem "Casey at the Bat" by Ernest Lawrence Thayer. It begins:

"The outlook wasn't brilliant for the Mudville nine that day;
The score stood four to two, with but one inning to play,
And then when Cooney died at first, and Barrows did the same,
A pall-like silence fell upon the patrons of the game."

I can relate to that "pall-like silence". I felt it every second as I walked to the batter's box and stood there with my bat on my shoulder. And that feeling lasted for many years. I felt it again, even more deeply, at my college orientation.

As the poem progresses, however, it goes in a very different direction than my youthful experience. Thayer wrote:

"There was ease in Casey's manner as he stepped into his place;
There was pride in Casey's bearing and a smile lit Casey's face.
And when, responding to the cheers, he lightly doffed his hat,
No stranger in the crowd could doubt 'twas Casey at the bat."

That wasn't my experience at all. But at this point Casey's story gets really interesting. With two strikes against him, and everything on the line, Casey knows that it all depends on him:

"The sneer is gone from Casey's lip, his teeth are clenched in hate,
He pounds with cruel violence his bat upon the plate;
And now the pitcher holds the ball, and now he lets it go,
And now the air is shattered by the force of Casey's blow."

He took the *swing*! With so much force that the air was "shattered." That's power. That's amazing. I find myself holding my breath.

I know he struck out. I've read the poem before. But still, I find myself in awe. He took the *swing* with *all his might*. He gave it everything. Okay, he struck out. Just like me. And he lost the game, while in my story we won. So a lot of things are different.

But one thing is incredibly different. One little thing. *He took the swing, with all his heart and soul.*

That's what it means to have courage. That's why he was such a famous hitter. That's why the crowd was so sure he would win it for them. Not because he was perfect. He clearly had his failures. The whole poem is about one of his huge failures. But he was a great and successful hitter because he took the *swing*. How many times he hit the ball isn't mentioned in the poem, but it must have been a lot or the fans wouldn't have been so sure of him.

Obviously Casey hit a lot of balls before this famous strike out, and no doubt he kept swinging in games that came later. Because of such swings, he was known as a truly great hitter. It isn't just the hits that bring success, *it's also the swings*. When we truly *swing* for what we want in life, with courage and our whole heart, we're going to get some big hits. But it is the swinging that counts.

Keeping the bat on my 12-year-old shoulder was the problem. Striking out while swinging would have been great. Way better than not even trying. And going to my college orientation alone, even fearful and doubting, would have been the right move too. The worst-case scenario is to not even *swing*, or to take mommy to hold my hand on the first day of college—to let fear run my life, instead of just trying. *Giving in to fear is worse than failure.*

PRINCIPLE 3

ACT

GIVING IN TO FEAR IS WORSE THAN FAILURE. COURAGEOUS ACTION IS VITAL FOR SUCCESS.

(Allowing fear to run our lives nearly always brings more and more fear. Trying and failing at least teaches us important lessons that help us learn how to do better.)

Failure is just failure; after all, it's not the end of the world. Everyone fails. And failure teaches us a lot of important lessons, if we're willing to learn from it. All truly successful people—in all walks of life—have failed and learned, and then kept trying. This is part of success. A key part. Just look at the string of failures put together by people like Abraham Lincoln, Winston Churchill, and Albert Einstein, all before they did truly great things.

Churchill said that "Success consists of going from failure to failure without loss of enthusiasm." Allowing fear to run our lives is much worse than failure, because it guarantees that we won't succeed. Letting fear control us shuts down enthusiasm, and it blocks our progress. That's the bottom of the barrel.

THE ZONE

Again, courage is the foundation of all success. And true success is found outside of your current reality, beyond your comfort zone. But here is the real question: Are you really comfortable in your comfort zone, or is your current place in life just *familiar?* For example, it would have been very easy for me to keep being a mechanic, staying in a safe place working for family and just barely getting by.

Getting stuck in one's comfort zone is probably the number one reason people do not get as far in life as they want to and could. Yes, I should have taken a *swing* at those pitches. And I should have heeded the advice to "man up" and gone alone to my college orientation. These would have pushed me beyond my comfort zone, to be sure, but they would have been better than what I did.

Of course, this is easier said than done. It's one thing to know that we need courage to live our dreams, but it's another thing entirely to muster one's courage and take action—even when we're scared, overwhelmed, and feel alone.

I knew I needed more courage—knew it for many years. I wanted to have more courage. I wished I had more courage. But wishing isn't the same as doing or having. My voices of inner doubt and fear kept telling me that I just didn't have much courage, and I listened to them.

EUREKA!

This is where the first big breakthrough occurred. I told you earlier that something changed in my life, and that this change catapulted me from fear to courage. It didn't happen all at once, but one thing did get it started. And knowing how to get your courage to start working in your mind and heart, even just a little bit, is really important. Once we're on the path to courage, it's easier to make progress. But until we start down this path, courage just seems to elude us, over and over and over. At least that's what I experienced.

So what caused the breakthrough? The truth is, this surprised me when it happened, and it still surprises me whenever I think about it today, even though many years have passed. I think the fact that what happened was so unexpected is one of the reasons it took me so long to do something about it. I just had no idea what was needed to be courageous. When I stumbled on it by accident… well, it changed everything. Like in Robert Frost's poem *The Road Not Taken*, when I learned what to do and started doing it—it changed my whole life. "And that has made all the difference," as Frost put it.

Specifically: dreams push you outside your comfort zone. Maybe something else can do this too, but for me it was my dreams. I have always been a big dreamer. Pictures

> **Specifically: dreams push you outside your comfort zone.**

of exotic cars filled my walls. I could name the make and model of a sports car just by the sound of it starting up and driving by. Big houses, land, ATVs—you name it, I wanted all the toys you can think of.

But until my breakthrough these were just dreams. I hoped they would somehow happen, but deep down I think I always assumed I wouldn't really turn them into reality—that I would just watch them go by like so many pitches in a baseball game. But then something changed. It started out so small…and then it drastically altered my entire life.

Here's what happened. I was 23, newly married, and the world was mine for the taking. At the time I was making about $9 per hour. Yep, I was on top of the world. I would drive into luxury car dealerships and tell my wife Lisa, "Someday I am going to get you a nice car." As I was saying these words we were driving cars with well over 150,000 miles on them. Both vehicles had multiple warning lights illuminated on the dash. To make things worse, I even needed to finance both of them.

Despite my promises, after three years of marriage, our first child already born, and now making a whopping $12 per hour, our lives weren't shaping up the way I had pictured in my head. The old voices of self-doubt kept nagging me, and I started to assume that I would never reach my dreams. I began to dismiss my desires as unrealistic ideas of my youth. I decided it was time to get my dreaming head out of the clouds and settle for living like everyone else around me, just barely making it, just getting by.

Don't get me wrong, things were okay, and we paid our bills. We had cable TV, played on sports leagues for fun, and took the once-a-year vacation up north to the Wisconsin Dells. I was settling into my comfort zone, still working for my step dad, while my wife Lisa ran a small daycare out of the lower level of our home. Things were good, I guess. But I couldn't shake the feeling that there was something more, that God did not plant the dreams in my heart to be forgotten, he planted them to be *attained*.

This discontent began to eat at me. Lisa and I started having conversations about building a larger daycare. We also began to brainstorm ways to improve the family repair shop, and to think about someday taking it over and running it. There had to be a way to live a bigger life, and to make a bigger impact.

I eventually decided to leave the family business and get a job at another dealership. It was my first "real" interview. I was terrified to be outside the comfort zone of our family business, but Lisa encouraged me to try. I attended the interview, and it went well. When the time came to discuss an offer, the person interviewing me threw out an amount. I was so afraid to speak, I froze and just sat there silent. He proceeded to make three more offers, without a word from me! He finally ended the interview with: "This is the best we can do. Let me know what you think."

Maybe I accidently fell upon a way to improve the outcomes of interviews: pure silence about anything financial! Later I accepted the job with almost a 100 percent increase in pay. However, on my first day I almost did not go because of fear. It took a lot of encouragement from Lisa to get me there. This was the first time my dream of a better life had pushed me out of my comfort zone. But I still wasn't fully living my dream.

At this point I was introduced to the opportunity of starting my own business. I was so excited at this prospect. It gave me hope that I could do something, a business that we could build in order to get where we wanted to go. There were doubts at first, a lot of them. It was a people business, and I did not like people. It was a leadership business as well, and I didn't feel like a leader. I struggled with a lot fear about the business. But I kept arguing with myself. "Yes, it's scary, but if Lisa would do it we could be free!"

I found that my dream was alive and well, with one small problem. I had big dreams on one side, and a small image of myself on the other. The only obstacle stopping me was a lack of courage to become, a lack of courage to change my story and win.

The inner voices of doubt and self-criticism increased their attacks in my mind: "I'm scared of everything. I was afraid to *swing*, afraid to make phone calls, afraid to go to college, and afraid to even ask my future wife out on a date. How could I possibly do this?"

The prospect of building my own business was a chance to relive and rescript my biggest failures, to step up to the plate again and *swing* this time, to push past the fear and go to orientation without my mom, to get on the phone and call—to not let my fears drive me. And this time was a lot like all the other times: So many fears and inner doubts kept me thinking about all the ways I could fail.

But this time something was a bit different.

WORTH FIGHTING

I fought back.

It's a little thing, really. But it turned out to be huge.

I only fought back in my thoughts, at first. But I pushed back. I didn't control my thoughts very well. I was beset by negativity, by doubts, by fears. But I did something I had never fully done before. For every negative thought, I pushed back with positive possibilities. To every inner doubt, I responded in my mind with words of potential. I felt a lot of fear, but I pushed back with words of enthusiastic excitement about what could happen.

I don't remember all the specific words of this great inner battle, but it went something like the following: "You can't do this," the old voice said. I replied in my mind: "If I do this, it will change our lives and we'll live our dreams. This is worth doing. It's time to take a stand."

When the old voice warned me that I wasn't the kind of person who hits home runs or wins games, I found something in my mind pointing out that I want to be that kind of person—immediately. And that now is the time to get started being that type of person.

> **There is so much power in a fight. And the greatest fight of our lives is found in our own mind.**

I'm not sure how it happened, but my inner dialogue changed. I wanted this dream so badly, and I found myself giving as much time and energy to what I wanted as to my fears. When the old voice told me I would be a failure if I tried to do this, I told it that not swinging the bat and not going alone to my college orientation had turned out horribly. "What do you know!" I asked the voice. "You've gotten it wrong my whole life. Listening to you is ridiculous."

These two sides of me battled and struggled. Only this time, the positive side kept fighting back. There is so much power in a fight. And the greatest fight of our lives is found in our own mind. When the old voice of self-doubt knocked me down, over and over, I did something different: I punched back.

How? This is the surprising thing I told you about, the breakthrough that changed everything in my life. Put simply: There was a tiny seed of courage in me—not full-blown courage, just a seed— and I started letting it talk. I let it have a voice. I didn't yet have the wisdom to fully reject the voices of fear and self-attack, but I let the seed of courage say as much as these other voices. Whatever they said, the seed talked back. It didn't win at first, but I let it talk anyway.

PRINCIPLE 4

MENTORS

AT SOME POINT, YOU HAVE TO LET THE SEED OF COURAGE INSIDE YOU HAVE A VOICE.

(You don't even have to believe this voice, at first. You don't have to let it win yet against other inner voices of doubt and fear. But you have to stop refusing to listen to this seed of courage, and you have to let it talk. Let it have its say, even if you reject what it says later. Just let it speak at least as much and as often as the voices of fear and doubt. Let the voice of courage—inside you and from others—become your greatest mentor.)

Between your current life and achieving your true dreams there are obstacles, challenges, even pitfalls. You will have critics to confront, habits to break and others to build, changes that need to be made, and struggles to overcome. You'll even have to endure and suffer some things.

To get where you want to go, you will have to draw upon the courage that is within. Winners always have to find what's stopping them and kick it out of the way. This will become a strength, over time, if you keep doing it.

Winners always have to find what's stopping them and kick it out of the way. This will become a strength, over time, if you keep doing it.

But to begin this process, you just have to do something very, very simple. Let the seed of courage that is already in you have a voice. Let it talk. Listen to it. Hear what it has to say. It's in there, trying to speak. Always. Right now.

You don't have to start by doing anything big or momentous. Just take a moment and find that seed of courage inside you, and ask it what it has to say to you.

Then listen.

It might surprise you. But don't argue with it right away. Believe me, your inner voices of doubt, fear, and criticism will almost certainly try to respond as loudly as they can. You won't silence them by just listening to your seed of courage. Don't worry that these negative voices will be lost—don't be afraid that they'll go away forever and you'll be worse off without them. They won't. They'll come back. But most of us rarely listen to our inner voice of courage.

The real problem for me, and for many people, is that over the years I had almost entirely silenced the little voice of courage within me. I had rejected, bullied, ignored and shut it down so often that I no longer even knew it was there.

Until I did.

CHANGE EVERYTHING!

When I let my dream in and found the seed of courage speaking up about building my business, I was very surprised. But the more I allowed it to speak, the more I realized that the real me was trying to break free. The more I allowed the voice of courage to speak, the more obvious it became that my seed of courage—not the voices of fear, doubt, and self-criticism—really knew me, knew who I am, and who I want to be. The voice of seedling courage knew what God wanted for me.

If you're not sure what your hidden voice of courage has to say, or even where it is buried away after so long, just ask yourself what your true dreams are in this life. If you were given all the time and money to do whatever you truly want, what would you do? Ask your seed of courage what dreams you would pursue if you weren't afraid of anything.

I promise, your voice of courage has something very important to tell you.

When I started noticing this voice, and listening, my whole life changed. You don't have to do this perfectly, just start listening to your voice of courage. And anytime you think a negative or fearful thing, ask your seed of courage what it thinks about the situation as well.

Then listen.

As I said, this was a little thing at first. But it changed everything. If you don't listen to the little voice of courage in your heart and mind, you won't exhibit much courage in life. But if you do start listening, even a little, it's truly amazing what can happen.

As successful entrepreneur Dan Waldschmidt said: "Controlling your thoughts is the hardest part of struggling toward success. There is nothing more difficult. No bigger challenge. And frankly, nothing more important."[1] Here's why this is such a big deal:

> Those who don't control their thoughts end up listening mostly to the wrong voices—fear, failure, give up, etc. And they believe what they hear. People who achieve success in anything must first learn to overcome this tendency and instead listen closely and frequently to their inner voice of courage. It's there. Hear what it has to tell you. Then keep focusing on it and listening.

When you do this, things will change for you. Without it, you'll never live your dreams. This is the raw truth. Every person who has attained great success can affirm this reality. That voice of courage is in you, just waiting to help you.

What does it want to tell you?

When I finally gave my tiny little seed of courage a voice, my whole life changed. Robert Frost said it perfectly: "Two roads diverged in a wood, and I—I took the one less traveled by..."

Like flipping a switch on a train track, this one decision redirected me toward a whole new life. I became a very different person. Today I am living my dreams—in marriage, family, faith, finances and leadership. Of course, there was more to it than this one decision. A lot more. But without the switch, without noticing the little voice of courage and listening, I would have stayed in that same rut, bat on shoulder, the spark missing in my eyes.

Fortunately, just listening to a seed of courage and giving it a voice created a breakthrough, a turning point, a new life purpose. And as I kept listening, I naturally moved toward the next step.

RECAP

- Giving into fear is worse than failure, because trying and failing nearly always teaches important lessons that help you improve.
- Courage is the foundation of all success; there is no true success without courage.
- The foundation of courage is the seed of courage that is found within each and every person.
- At some point, people who succeed in life learn to notice the seed of courage within them and listen to it.
- Successful people develop the habit of letting the inner voice of courage respond to any negative thoughts, feelings and voices, and to trust the voice of courage above these other voices.
- When a person does this, he/she nearly always experiences a breakthrough, a potential turning point in life, a call to live his or her dreams.

CHAPTER 2

THE COURAGE TO DREAM BIG

"All our dreams can come true,
if we have the courage to pursue them."
—Walt Disney

Lisa and I stayed up nearly all night talking about the possibilities. A long list of positive "what ifs…" rolled though my mind. I tossed and turned, trying to sleep, but my dreams kept me from drifting off. I felt like a child again, the possibilities seemed endless. My own company, the thought of good money, travel, nice homes, cars, the ability to give to others. My head was full of dreams and, for the moment, no limits.

The next morning I woke up and to my surprise the dreams were still on my mind, hope still in my heart. This was it, a chance to do something big. A new voice in my mind kept telling me that I was up to this, that we could do it. *Yes, it will be hard work,* the voice of courage assured me, *but it will be worth it. And you can do this. It's time.*

I also had my doubts. The old voice of discouragement made sure of that. But anytime the old voice spoke out, I thought about what the voice of courage had to say as well. And, funny thing, courage turned out to be stronger and smarter than fear. This happened over and over. Courage started winning.

WHAT'S POSSIBLE?

But I'm getting ahead of myself. Let's back up to the beginning. The night before, someone stopped over at our house to share a business plan with us. Not just any plan, but the very business plan that would eventually lead Lisa and I to participate in the start of a multi-million dollar company and create the life we enjoy so much today. We didn't realize it at the time, but our dreams were sitting at the kitchen table talking to us.

As the plan was being shared, I felt a stir in my heart. I had never felt quite this way before. It was as if a true calling was being offered. Now to be fair, that night I wasn't sure what I was feeling. To this point in our life I had pretty much just sat back and let Lisa lead the house and make most of the decisions. She had a strong personality and I...well, I struggled.

I remember very clearly the night she called to say she had made an appointment to look at a business. She said I needed to be home at 7 o'clock on Thursday for the meeting she had set up. This caused a couple of problems right off the bat. First, I wanted nothing to do with some home-based business. I'd heard it all before, and it just wasn't my thing. Or so I thought.

Second, it was Thursday night, meaning that "Must See TV" was on. I am probably dating myself here, but back then the slogan for the network was "Thursday Night Must See TV." We accepted this motto and lived it. Every Thursday we faithfully watched TV for about four hours. It was a highlight of the week for me: from *Friends* to *ER*, what a night! How dare Lisa suggest we skip "Must See TV!" That will ruin my week, I thought.

Looking back from where we are now this seems nothing short of absurd, but that is where we were. In any case, I wasn't buying it. I was frustrated and upset. And for maybe the first time in our married life I decided to step up and take charge of an event. I told her I wasn't going to attend. Instead, I informed her, if I couldn't watch my weekly dose of Thursday-night escape, I would at the very least do something important by staying at work late and putting in some overtime. "We could use the extra money this month," I told her.

To all of this Lisa firmly responded: "Oh yes you are coming to this meeting, and you will be home before 7 so you can shower." I took a deep breath, and then I slowly slid right back into my normal posture and said, "Yes, Dear."

Now just to be clear, Lisa was not mean or out of line in any way, it was just that up to this point in our life she had made most of these kinds of decisions for us because I had so little confidence. But guess what? God has a wonderful way of making things happen in our life. I did come home before 7 that night, we did skip "Must See TV," and it changed our lives forever.

The impact of this one choice has been huge. For example, there's a popular view that people who get a bachelor's degree earn about a million dollars more in life than those who don't, and even though this statistic has been debunked[2] a lot of people still believe

The impact of this one choice has been huge.

it. But here's the "statistic" I know to be true: If I had skipped the meeting that night, it would have cost us many, many millions of dollars. That's not theory, it's reality. This is how significant that business meeting was for us.

TWO PATHS

I think most people can remember a time when hope began to flow into their life, when a better future suddenly seemed like a possibility. When this happens, everything around you looks new, fresh and within your reach. Why then, do so many people stop at hope and never make the changes to act on and reach their dreams? What causes us to bury these feelings and fall back into our comfort zone (or, more accurately, our zone of familiarity)?

Here is the trick, which we learned from great mentors who helped Lisa and I take the "idea" of building a successful business and turn it into a reality. This takes a lot of work, sweat and tears. But, as our mentors told us early on in this process, the results make the hard work worth it. I was already working hard at the repair shop, and Lisa was certainly working hard with our daycare business.

The difference is that this path would never have gotten us much beyond the month-to-month grind of just breaking even, while the other path, the entrepreneurial approach, allowed us to live our dreams. Both of these required hard work, but the results of the two were very different.

I've noticed over the years that a lot of people work very hard, but not everyone gets the kind of compensation that successful entrepreneurs do. I wanted to take this path, but I wasn't sure how to do it. Fortunately, several mentors, including people like Eric

Blomdahl, George Guzzardo, Orrin Woodward, and others, taught us what to do. And we followed what they taught us.

PRINCIPLE 5

CHANGE

NOTHING BOOSTS YOUR COURAGE LIKE WORKING CLOSELY WITH A MENTOR (OR MENTORS) WHO HAS ALREADY ACHIEVED SUCCESS IN THE THING YOU ARE TRYING TO ACCOMPLISH. THIS IS THE PATH OF CHANGE THAT TRULY BRINGS SUCCESS.

(Such mentors already have firsthand experience with courage, listening to the seed of courage within, and helping you understand what to do, avoid, stop, start, and emphasize. If you try to figure this all out on your own by trial and error, you're usually setting yourself up for way too many mistakes. One of the most effective ways to succeed is simple: find and learn from successful mentors.)

MENTORS CAN MAKE THE DIFFERENCE

The truth is that the people we associate with have great influence on our thinking, our courage or lack of it, and whether or not we succeed. For example, in the classic baseball movie *For the Love of the Game*, the lead character, played by Kevin Costner, faces an uphill battle as he tries to rehabilitate himself after an injury. All the odds are against him ever returning to play baseball again. During this process, one of the people close to him expresses doubts about his ability to reach his goals.

He immediately tells the person, a physical trainer, to either get his head right or stop being around him. He knows that the people we spend time with make all the difference. The trainer changes his attitude, and the main character succeeds in coming back to the game—in fact, he is even better than before the injury. But he couldn't have done this without keeping his thinking focused on the voice of courage, and he knew that the voices of the people he associates with deeply matter. Such voices often make the difference between success and something less.

Indeed, throughout the movie, whenever Costner's character is on the pitching mound and wants to focus on the right voices in his mind and achieve real success, he repeats to himself the words: "Clear the Mechanism." This is a mental trigger he has taught himself to use to replace all negative voices with the right voice. I know a number of successful people who do the same thing. For example, one of my mentors uses the term "Fired Up" to keep focused on the voice of courage in his life, and a friend of mine uses the phrase "Switch Up" to remind himself to look to Heaven and the voice of courage instead of trusting the lower voices of the world. Another possible trigger to focus your mind on the voice of courage could be "*Swing!*"

The trigger I use is "You Win." I know everything has a solution if I stay focused. It's as if I record a game on Sunday and plan to watch it on Monday. Let's say I avoid everyone who saw the game, knowing I don't want to hear the outcome before watching it. However, someone slips up and tells me that my team won

8-5. I watch the game anyway, and in the third inning my team is down 5-0!

Knowing the outcome of the game, however, I'm not depressed, or even worried. In fact, I'm fired up! I can't wait to see how this ends. It must be awesome. I am so excited to watch the come back! This is similar to focusing on the voice of courage.

During times of struggle as we built our business, I would tell myself, "Dan, you already know how this ends. You win." This trigger would stop me from focusing on the struggle and help me look toward my future.

Every time I used it, my attitude immediately improved and I pivoted directly to the voice of courage. I use this phrase still, a lot.

Again: If you want to achieve your goals, replace all fear-based voices with the voice of courage, and also remove any associations with people that drag you down and replace them with people who listen to and encourage the voice of courage. In our case, we simply could not have achieved the success we have experienced without the help of great mentors. They have made a huge difference in our work.

In fact, it was one of these mentors who taught me that I must give the voice of courage more focus than the voices of fear or self-doubt. And he taught me specifically how to do this. It's really very simple: Whenever you have self-defeating thoughts or feelings, stop, recognize that you're letting these voices influence you, and then focus on listening to the inner voice of courage. Take notes on what your seed of courage tells you to do. Never let your critical self-talk drown out courage. Always listen to what courage has to say. Always.

This theme is further developed in the book *The Ant and the Elephant* by author Vince Poscente. He compares our conscious and subconscious minds to an ant (the conscious mind) running on the back of an elephant (our subconscious). The ant talks to the elephant, and the elephant listens. The thing is, we have total control of our conscious mind, what the ant tells the elephant, at any given moment. We can tell it we have courage, talent, and ability, or we can tell it we are losers, destined to fail in life.

> **We can tell our subconscious that we have courage, talent, and ability, or we can tell it we are losers, destined to fail in life.**

If our ant is constantly telling our elephant that we are losers and failures, it starts to believe it, and it moves in that direction. After years of convincing our subconscious of these negatives, we can't just suddenly announce to the elephant that we are actually winners and destined to succeed. Or, more precisely, we can try to tell the elephant this new information, but it takes a lot for an ant to stop an elephant's momentum.

After the ant tells the elephant one thing millions of times, or with a lot of intense emotion, the elephant pretty much believes it and acts on it. In my case, I had been telling myself for years that I was a failure, destined to let fear run my life, and my ant had convinced my elephant of this lie.

When I learned to give the seed of courage inside me a voice, my ant started telling my elephant about it. Of course, this didn't change my subconscious immediately. But it started to give my subconscious mind (elephant) a different view of things. Over time, my mentors taught me, I needed to give little or no credence to self-doubt and self-lies, and use my conscious thoughts (the ant) to keep teaching my elephant "the truth."

This really worked, but it wasn't easy or immediate. It was simple, however. At first, as mentioned earlier, I learned to just give my inner courage a voice, to listen to it, to let it speak. Then, once I was doing this, my mentors taught me to replace the self-defeating voices in my mind with the voice of courage. Successful people make this a habit, and they are very serious about it and totally committed to it. Some do it naturally, and others do it more consciously, but this is something all truly successful people do.

PRINCIPLE 6

GROW

IN EVERY MOMENT, REPLACE ALL SELF-DEFEATING SELF-TALK WITH THE VOICE OF COURAGE. THIS IS THE PATH OF GROWTH.

(Make this a habit. Focus on always doing this. If you start struggling again with self-defeating self-talk, refocus on this principle.)

When you're only listening to courageous self-talk, you tend to act with a lot more courage. Most people don't realize how powerful this is. Yes, it can be challenging to change our mental habits, but when we do, we realize how much power we have to hurt ourselves, block our own progress, or help ourselves succeed.

The funny thing about this principle is that a lot of people like to attack it, or laugh at it. I guess this makes sense, since some people take the idea to an extreme, such as the concept that sitting around all day thinking positively can magically control the whole world or force God to acquiesce to your wants. Obviously, that's too extreme. And untrue.

When you're only listening to courageous self-talk, you tend to act with a lot more courage.

But let's get real. Spending most of our lives with negative, self-critical, and self-defeating thoughts doesn't do us much good. It only hurts us. In contrast, putting aside self-defeating thoughts and focusing on wise, positive, creative, and self-improving self-talk really does increase our productivity, effectiveness, and happiness. It also helps increase our courage.

If we allow our thoughts to emphasize the self-image of loser, failure, powerless, we'll tend to live this way. If we consistently replace these thoughts with the dreams, talents, and opportunities God has given us, we're a lot more likely to do better and bigger things in life.

The evidence is overwhelming. Find a person who is truly successful in any walk of life, and you'll find a person who has learned to more effectively control his or her thoughts—at least in the area where he has achieved success. Self-defeating thoughts lead to self-defeat. And while self-supporting thoughts alone don't bring success, they are at least a vital part of effectively achieving our goals.

DREAMS > OBSTACLES?

My mentors also taught me something else that is very important to success. To put it simply: if you want to get past your fears and truly obtain your goals, you must get your dreams bigger than your obstacles.

PRINCIPLE 7

QUESTION

GET YOUR DREAMS BIGGER THAN YOUR OBSTACLES.

(If your obstacles are bigger than your dreams, you won't do what is needed to get past them. You'll eventually give up or otherwise stop pursuing your dreams. Ask questions: Are your dreams what they should be? Are they big enough? Are they bigger than the obstacles? If not, why not?)

As one of my mentors, Orrin Woodward, is famous for saying: "When the pain of staying the same gets bigger that the pain of change, you will change." It really is that simple. Not easy, but simple. Another mentor taught me that if all you see is your obstacles, they are all you will ever have.

> **"When the pain of staying the same gets bigger that the pain of change, you will change."**
> **—Orrin Woodward**

Think about that for a moment.

To get past our fears and achieve our dreams in life, we need to get a dream that is big enough to catapult us over (and often through) our obstacles. A quote that sticks in my head, though I'm not sure where it came from, is: "Focus on what you are going to, not what you are going through."

For example, at one point in our life our finances were out of control. Our expenses were more than our income and every month we were falling further behind. Debt was beginning to mount, and my positive outlook started failing. One day it hit me while I was listening to an audio: "All I think about is my debt and problems. If I continue to make these my focus, I will just have more of the same."

At that moment I replaced my fears with the voice of courage and asked myself: "What business goal would I need to hit to get ahead financially, pay off all our debts, and have money in the bank for a change?" That night I wrote out my goals and printed them in big letters, then I posted them on the ceiling above my side of the bed. Lisa was not impressed, at least not at first.

But everyday I would wake up and then later go to sleep thinking about the goals we were going toward, not about the struggles we were going through. Not long after this (though it was long enough to do a lot of very hard work), we hit our goal, paid off our debt, and for the first time had 5 figures in our bank account after we paid all the bills. The reality is that you may not get what you want in life, but you will always get what you focus on!

The more I focused on my problems, the bigger they got. When I finally focused on my goals, they became real.

On a personal note, as mentioned, I had a lot of fear of people, and I had piles of subconscious and conscious doubts based on my past. However, when I thought about my dreams in life, the fear of not obtaining a better future was bigger that the fear of people. It really was.

So I changed. I had to. It was painful, yes. But not as painful as giving up on my dream.

For the first few years of building our business, we struggled. I kept working at the repair shop, and then we worked on the business in the evenings and weekends. It was often difficult, and numerous times I wanted to quit. But each time this came up I realized I was at a crossroads. Was I going to let fear keep me where I was in life, or find a way to develop the courage to become?

Just the act of dreaming requires courage. When you begin to let your mind and subconscious dream, something crazy happens. You automatically begin ask questions like the following:

- Can I really do this?
- Is it actually possible to pursue and attain my dreams?
- Will this all be a waste of time, money and effort, or can it really happen?

This is where so many people stop. The fear of not getting their dreams overwhelms their level of belief. I've seen this way too many times. People give up on what they were truly meant to do and become because fear gets in their way. Most people never make it past this point; the inner critic is so strong it overcomes the inner dreamer. When fear is bigger than hope, the person doesn't allow the seed of courage to lead.

> **The fear of not getting their dreams overwhelms their level of belief.**

GREATEST OF ALL

This pattern—all too human, and all too widespread—reminds me of a story I once heard. A man passes away and finds himself in heaven. While waiting to meet God he looks around the room and sees a large throng of people waiting with him. He speaks to one of the attendants of Heaven, and during the conversation he points to a man in the corner and asks the attendant: "Who is that?"

"That is the greatest general who ever lived," the official replies.

"Wow! What's his name?" the man asks.

When the attendant tells him the general's name, the man shakes his head in confusion. "I've never heard of him," he confesses. "If he is the greatest general who ever lived, why don't I know his name?"

A bit surprised by the man's candor, the attendant replies: "Maybe I should clarify. He had the greatest innate ability and talent for generalship of anyone who ever lived. If he would have exercised the courage to become a general, he *would* have been the greatest general who ever lived! He just didn't end up doing it. He got scared."

"Oh," the man replied. No doubt he then looked around and wondered what he was doing in this particular room. "Is this the room for people with undeveloped potential?"

I believe all of us are meant to do something special, our great life purpose on this earth. However, at some point many of us realize what we should do or be but lack the courage to fully pursue it. Too many of us settle for something less.

As we've already discussed, the first step to living your dreams is gaining the courage to succeed by overcoming your inner critic and other self-defeating self-talk. From the surface this seems like such an easy thing to do. But everyone who has achieved real success in life, in whatever field or focus, knows just how tough this can be. I know from personal experience that I was always harder on myself than anybody else. In fact, if anyone in my life spoke to me the way I used to speak to myself, I may not ever speak to him or her again!

PUTTING COURAGE IN CHARGE

As we built our business, this battle continued. The more I dreamed and planned, the more the old critical voice would say: "Who do you think you are? You aren't one of the 'Nates' of this world, you should just leave the bat on your shoulder and stay average." I learned to turn to my inner voice of courage and let him respond. Imagine our discussion: "Actually, I'm not the little 12-year-old Danny that you can bully. I *swing* the bat now, and even though sometimes I still strike out, a lot of the time I hit the ball, including some home runs and even grand slams. But I'm too busy to listen to you right now." Then I focus on the important things of the day.

No matter how bad you once were (or now are) at this battle, you can reach the point where your inner voice of courage runs your life—instead of the self-defeating voices. The inner critic is always around, trying to make mischief, but you can become very skilled at replacing that voice with the voices that really matter.

During this time of working hard each day to make a living and then working even harder every evening to build our business, it is interesting how staying average was both my comfort zone and my biggest fear. In my heart I knew I was not meant to be average, but too often my mind would only recall times that highlighted my weaknesses. That's how powerful the subconscious (elephant) can be. I just keep feeding it the truth, however, by turning to my voice of courage and listening.

One of my favorite songs at this point in life was "Voice of Truth" by Casting Crowns. The music and lyrics helped me remember to always listen to the inner voice of courage, not some other voice. If I ever felt down, overwhelmed, or defeated, this song helped me refocus on the right voice.

> **My mentors had taught me to do this—always listen to the voice of courage, not other voices.**

My mentors had taught me to do this—always listen to the voice of courage, not other voices—and I learned the same lesson by reading books and listening to audios from great leaders. This habit is key to success. It is a vital part of overcoming the wrong voices and focusing on the voice of courage.

Put simply, the right kind of Reading, Listening, and Associating are crucial. Since the crux of the battle between the voice of courage and other, damaging, voices is fought in the mind, what we read, what we listen to, and the people we associate with drastically influence how well we do in this war for our own mind. The good news is that, knowing this, we can choose to specifically read the kinds of things that help the voice of courage win. Likewise, we can wisely choose to listen to audios that greatly strengthen the voice of courage, and associate with people who are living with the voice of courage as the dominant voice in their lives. This is incredibly important.

I took this very seriously. One of the blessings of being an auto mechanic was the many hours I spent with myself.. Now I say blessing, but this can also be a curse. When your thinking is off, time alone can be very damaging. Fighting the inner critic can be quite a battle. The good news is, I had plenty of time to listen to audios from people who focus on the voice of courage. My co-workers would have a radio blasting the classic rock station or the latest morning show hosts. I very quickly realized that was not feeding my mind as well as I wanted.

So everyday I would grab my Walkman (yes, I am dating myself) and a pile of audios. Listening to anywhere from 1 to 8 hours of positive information a day is really helpful. The most powerful thing about this is that when good information is going into your brain, it is hard for the inner critic to speak. I learned to drown out the inner critic with positive information.

I will warn you: this can be a little dangerous! One time I was deep into a talk and hanging on every word. I was leaning over a running engine looking for a coolant leak. I typically only put in one ear bud at a time so I could be safe and still hear my surroundings. The other half of the ear buds where tucked into my shirt pocket. But on this occasion, the ear bud slipped out of my shirt pocket and fell into the fan blades. Instantly the force of the fan grabbed the cable which was attached to my Walkman and ripped it out of my pants pocket, sending it flying across the shop only to smash into multiple pieces!

Another great source of positive information that really helps change your thinking and defeat the inner critic is reading great books. Now to this point in my life I only read things like trade journals and magazines. I had not read a book since high school, but realized this was a powerful way to win the battle of the mind.

For example, one of the first books I ever remember reading in one sitting was *An Enemy Called Average* by John Mason. The book arrived one day as part of my business reading, suggested by my mentors, and for some reason the title immediately grabbed my attention. Once I started reading, I couldn't put it down. It spoke directly to my heart, as if the author wrote it just for me. Here is how the book starts:

"Mediocrity is a region bound on the North by compromise, on the South by indecision, on the East by past thinking, and on the West by lack of vision."

Wow! This hit home. As I read, I realized that the book was helping me change the negative narrative of my long-term inner voice, and it helped me develop the courage to dream big. I found that one of the quickest and most effective ways to retrain my brain from loser-thinking to winner-thinking was to fill it with words, thoughts, and stories from other people who have fought this same battle and effectively replaced the inner-critic with the voice of courage.

Books, articles, speeches, audios—wherever great ideas can be found, they are worth pursuing. Knowledge is power, as the old saying goes. But there is actually more to it than that: The right kind of knowledge also catalyzes courage.

PRINCIPLE 8

OVERCOME FAILURE

FAILURE WILL HAPPEN. IT IS PART OF ANY PATH TO SUCCESS.

LISTENING TO STORIES, SPEECHES, AND AUDIOS THAT TEACH ABOUT COURAGE, AND READING BOOKS AND ARTICLES THAT DO THE SAME, INCREASES ONE'S ABILITY TO STAY FOCUSED ON THE INNER VOICE OF COURAGE RATHER THAN THE INNER CRITIC, EVEN AFTER FAILURES OCCUR.

(If the inner critic ever starts influencing you, you probably aren't giving enough time to the right kind of reading and listening.)

OUTER CRITICS

Another reason we all need courage to dream is that most people don't aim for their best. This is surprising, when you think about it. Too often we humans simply settle for much less than we could, or should. This kind of unfulfilling fake-contentment has reached the level of a cultural norm in some communities, families, and other groups. To overcome this, we not only have to find our courage, but also realize that it's even worth seeking in the first place.

For example, the morning after that 7 o'clock Thursday business meeting, I headed back to work. I was still feeling positive, but I quickly learned that I wasn't the only one who could doubt my abilities. When I started telling other people about our plans to build an entrepreneurial business and live our dreams, things really started to get tough. I thought they'd be happy for me. Boy was I wrong. Most of the people I told about our new plan quickly took it upon themselves to convince me to drop my "big ideas" immediately.

> We live in a world were most people chose to survive instead of thrive. They are bound in mediocrity, with no sense that they could truly do better.

Put another way: We live in a world where most people choose to survive instead of thrive. They are bound in mediocrity, with no sense that they could truly do better. But this unhealthy and tragic viewpoint often devolves into something even worse: the attempt to keep others from doing better as well. In fact, it baffles me that so many people are not only content with not pursuing their dreams, but also feel the need to discourage you from going after yours.

This is shocking, and sad. Such people feel it is their personal mission to tell you how they have failed at attaining their dreams so they can save you the pain of trying to live yours. They want to convince you to settle for less, to give up. I know that many of them are well intentioned, that they are truly trying to save you pain. But what is a victory without a struggle? Without the battle the achievement would be hollow.

I have had my share of failures in life, but I simply can't imagine trying to "help" other people avoid doing better. I can hardly conceive of walking toward the dugout after not even swinging at the pitches, only to stop Nate on his way to bat and trying to convince him to not *swing* either. "Hey Nate, just keep the bat on your shoulder, man. If you *swing*, you might miss. That would be such a failure. Everyone will think you're a loser. Just stand there and don't even try. Seriously. Just go strike out, and let's lose this game and head home. Be a pal!"

Never. It just doesn't make any sense to me. Yet I've seen so many people do basically the same thing. They see someone trying to step up and improve his or her life, and they take it upon themselves to talk that person out of even trying.

For example, when I was just getting started on my business, just mustering the courage to go out and act, one of the first people I decided to share my ideas with was a friend from high school. I remember being so excited to share my goals and dreams with him. I was sure he would jump on board with me and do something big. After a few days I tried calling him back to get together and move forward. By the third or fourth unanswered phone call, I realized something must be up.

A few days later I received an email from another high school friend saying something like this: "Hey Dan, just thought it was only fair to share this with you. I received the attached email from [our mutual friend]." Basically the email said: "Hey everyone, Dan has got some crazy idea for a business he is starting. If I were you I would not answer his calls, because he will try to sucker you in!"

Wow, that hurt! It turns out the email was sent to numerous high school friends to "warn" them about my big ideas.

My "true" friend in this case was the guy who shared this email with me. He was not interested in my business ideas but still encouraged me to pursue my dreams. That is a real friend, someone who may or may not join you, but still encourages your success.

Years later, at my twenty-year class reunion, both friends were positive, congratulated me on my success, and were proud of how many people we have helped succeed along the way. But things don't always have such a positive outcome. Too often, it seems, if you push past the negative attacks and do attain your dreams, it makes many of the naysayers even more uncomfortable.

A few get excited for you, and some even benefit from your example and do things to improve themselves as well, but most are more frustrated than ever. I think this happens because you have just proven that if they could find the courage they too could pursue and achieve their dreams. At some point in their lives they put their bats on their shoulders and decided it was too painful or difficult to try. And they've gotten used to being stuck in that place, even though they actually hate it.

Still, your example of success will help a lot of people, even some of those who start out as naysayers. To dream of a bigger life takes courage, as does confronting your inner doubts and enduring the slings and arrows of others.

During the early years of building our business, it was amazing how many people wanted to talk us out of it. But I learned something very important from all this: the next principle.

PRINCIPLE 9

ASSOCIATE

(With the right people, and the right voices.)

KEEP YOUR EYE ON THE REAL BATTLE: YOUR INNER THOUGHTS. WHAT OTHER PEOPLE SAY TO YOU, OR ABOUT YOU, ONLY BECOMES A ROADBLOCK IF YOU LISTEN TO YOUR INNER CRITIC.

(If you always replace your inner critic with the voice of courage, you'll handle what other people say efficiently and effectively. In fact, this process can greatly strengthen your courage and resolve. Associate more with people who follow the voice of courage.)

I'm not sure where I got this quote, but I've found it to be very true: "You can succeed in life if no one believes in you, but you will never succeed if you do not believe in yourself."

As I learned to effectively fight the great inner battle, I was surprised by how quickly I could go from picturing the future I always wanted to doubting myself again. When other people tried to convince me to give up on my dream and instead just be content with my car repair job and "Must See TV Thursday", I found myself struggling between two types of reactions.

TWO REACTIONS: ONE BAD, ONE GOOD

Reaction One: If I started worrying about their criticisms, my inner critic always joined in and I quickly started thinking things like:

- How can an auto mechanic ever become a successful business owner?
- Who am I to think I can actually lead people?
- Will I just waste my time and money pursuing my dreams? Should I just give up, get out my Visa, and go buy a bigger TV?

When I let these kinds of thoughts loop in my mind, sudden memories of my past rushed into my mind, "verifying" why I could "never succeed".

It is important to realize that every successful person has these kinds of thoughts to some extent. Those who learn how to truly succeed, however, don't let their inner critic join forces with the negative things people say. Instead, they take the second approach to dealing with such thoughts.

Reaction Two: The best method is to double down on replacing all self-defeating voices with the voice of courage. This is incredibly powerful. Whatever the critical person said to you, just let your courage deal with it. Not your inner critic, who will always steer you wrong.

This can be a little tricky, actually, because your inner critic speaks from a place of fear, and the first thing most of us fear when someone criticizes us is that he or she is right. "Maybe I really will fail, and fail spectacularly," our inner fear tells us. "Maybe this will

lead to even bigger failures…" Then our voice of fear starts imag-
ining all kinds of negative scenarios.

If we let this happen, it won't be long until our voices of fear and
self-criticism assure us of something along the lines of: soon we'll
go broke, be forced to live in a ditch, and our home will be hit by
an asteroid. Not just any asteroid, mind you, but a plague-infested
asteroid that only hits our family, and nobody else. And everyone
will see how we caused it with our stupid choice to…

As I said, the voice of fear lives for the ridiculous. That's just
how the voices of fear and self-criticism work. They lie. And they
lie creatively and passionately. They also exaggerate as they lie. Why
would we ever listen to them?

The truth is, successful people learn not to listen to them at all.
Instead, they listen to the voice of
courage. Courage isn't afraid to face
the truth, so if something the critics
said is actually real, it will tell you
so. "You need to improve on this,"
your voice of courage will assure
you. No judgment. No scary
scenarios about living in a ditch.
Just: "Fix this! And be thankful the critic pointed it out. Now you
can solve it. Let's get to work on this."

> **Those who learn how to truly succeed, however, don't let their inner critic join forces with the negative things people say.**

Likewise, the voice of courage will tell you if the critic was
wrong. If so, courage will suggest that you ignore it, or fight it
to set the record straight, or get more information, or do whatever you need to do. This is so much better than operating from a
place of fear. Courage simply says: "Problem? Okay, let's learn the
specifics. That's done? Great, now here's our best course of action."

TURN REJECTION INTO ENERGY

My very first phone call about becoming an entrepreneur was to my sister. I was so excited to share my ideas. My business coach at the time recommended calling my sister to book a time to sit down and talk with her. "This should only take about 45 seconds" my coach said, "just book an appointment and get off the phone. Do not try to explain the business plan over the phone!" Well, 45 minutes after she said "hello," after I tried to explain the business idea in detail, she said "No thanks" and hung up.

That would not have been terrible, but my next call was to my mom. When she picked up I quickly learned that my sister had already called her to give her the low down. As soon as my mom picked up the phone she said, "I am not interested. I have tried to start a business like that before, they never work."

That didn't go so well.

Over the next couple of years my close family members and I had many discussions about my business. It seemed like holiday gatherings were mainly designed as interventions to "help" Dan give up on his delusions of success in this type of endeavor. Everyone in my family seemed to be against my ideas of building this business. Some of my brothers and sisters joined me in the business, only to quit later because of the intensity of family opposition. It got so bad that at one point we had to make a family declaration: "No talking about my business at a family gathering, or we are not coming. Let's just agree to disagree and move on!"

This accomplished a couple things for me. My inner voice of courage said: "Dan, this is your chance to prove who you are. Both views of this can't be right. Either it will work for you and you will be right, or you will fail and they will be right. But the great thing is this: Who is right is entirely up to you!"

This drove me to succeed. I pasted a quote on my toolbox at the repair shop where I worked, and I read it every time I faced an outer critic. It read: "People of integrity expect to be believed, and when they are not, they let time and their actions prove them right."

It was truly up to me. Now the only question was: "Did I have the character to follow through?"

After making a decision to not attend family gatherings unless we did not discuss the business, things got a little better. I know my family only had my best interests at heart, but just because they had not succeeded in the past didn't mean that I couldn't succeed. Sometimes the people who love you most can give you the most grief at first. Not because they do not believe in you, but they are trying to protect you. From their perspective you are heading the wrong direction and they are only trying to save you pain. My mom deeply cared about me and wanted to help me; she really believed I would succeed, just not in this way.

But this is what I wanted. I had to keep the voice of courage in charge, or I easily got sucked into fearful thinking. As time went by, I began reading a lot more and listening to lots of audios. I frequently shared stories, principles, or quotes I was learning with my mom. She would say, "Where are you learning this stuff?"

"Well, in my business..."

"Stop, I don't want to hear about your business," she would say.

We had many great talks about leadership and self-improvement. My mom has amazing knowledge about this topic. She has overcome so many things in her past by learning to improve herself and grow. I knew if I could prove that my business worked and get her to see the bigger picture, she would love what we do.

Finally, after years like this, she started to crack. I announced in one of our conversations that Lisa was quitting her day job. We were making enough from our business; we no longer needed her income. Worried, Mom asked, "How can you afford that? I know what you make as a mechanic."

"Well, in my business..."

"Stop, I don't want to hear about your business!" she said.

This kind of dialogue went on for a long time.

Finally, one afternoon I stopped over at my mom's work and we were having a great conversation. She looked at me and said, "If I show you something, will you promise not to try to talk me into your business?" I just smiled and said, "Sure, what's up?"

She pulled out a piece of paper. At some point in her life she had read a book that recommended writing out your perfect day. As she read her plan for a perfect day, it described exactly what success looked like in "my business." I just smiled and walked out saying, "Man, I sure wish you wanted to hear about my business, I think you would love it!"

A while later, Lisa gave my mom a call and asked, "What are you doing Saturday night? It's Dan's birthday." Excited, my mom replied, "Nothing." She thought we were having a party of some sort. Lisa continued: "Great. Dan is speaking at a seminar and we would love for you to come and hear him speak!" She agreed to attend. Out of all of my siblings, I was the last one she had expected to speak on a stage. She had to come to see that! I had been so shy for so long—she could hardly believe I would give a speech.

I only had 10 minutes to speak, but that was enough. She saw something in me that night she had known was possible, but seemed so unlikely. That seminar changed everything for her. She enjoyed the other speakers, and liked the people she met. The biggest moment for her occurred when a young man approached her and asked if she was my mom. When she said yes, he proceeded to thank her for the impact her son was having on his life.

At that moment my mom embraced our business. Later she would get started on her own journey, working with us in business and impacting people as a leader. In fact, she loved what we were learning, but she still didn't believe we would make much money from it. Shortly after this I surprised Lisa by purchasing her an Escalade, her dream vehicle. I was telling my mom about this and she said, "Oh my, that is an expensive vehicle. How will you afford the payments?"

To which I replied: "What payments? I was able to pay cash!"

"How could you do that as a mechanic?"

When she learned that our business was working on a financial level, she became even more excited about it. Today, she and her husband have influenced so many people and teach from stages for our company, sharing their story and teaching leadership principles. Many other members of my family are involved and work together on the business. Happily, family gatherings are now a bit different as well.

The voice of courage brings solutions and answers to life's challenges. If you're still listening to the fear voice, however, you won't have any solutions. The fear voice is still spinning out of control. That's what the voice of fear does. It keeps telling you worse things (most of them entirely made up): "You will live in a ditch. Your spouse will live in a ditch. Your kids will live in a ditch. Probably your uncle will have to come live in the ditch with you."

This kind of looping on a negative voice or thought is known as "capture,"[3] where a false and extreme feeling or thought grabs our attention and keeps reasserting itself until it comes to dominate our perception.[4] This is not only unhealthy, it can take over our attention and distract us from what is important. It is, however, up to us whether or not we allow such looping to persist to this point.

As I said above, the inner voice of fear doesn't help you. Successful people become successful only when they learn to replace it with the voice of courage, and then take whatever action (or inaction) is best to deal with the situation. Courage has answers. It has solutions. In contrast, the voice of fear only has more fear to offer. Plus, it's still stuck in the ditch, except by now it's no ordinary ditch, it's an awful, horrid, smelly ditch. And it's muddy. And…

Wait. Waste of time. Replace that voice with the voice of courage.

"Oh, that feels nice. No more ditch? Excellent. What should I focus on next?"

Of course, every person's self-defeating voices have different fears. For you it might have nothing to do with failure, "living in a ditch", or looking bad to other people, but whatever your fears are, the voice of fear will exaggerate them and use them to hold you back—if it can. It is our job to take away this power from the voice of fear and give it to the voice of courage. This is a vital part of the path to success, for anyone and everyone.

THESE VOICES ARE REAL

Again, it is one thing to always replace your inner-critic and voice of fear with the voice of courage. This is a crucial beginning.

But it's a whole new level to do the same thing when someone criticizes, attacks, lies about you or those you love, tries to rain on your parade, or otherwise tries to tear you down—or even genuinely tries to help you by getting you to quit your dreams and settle for barely getting by.

But in both cases, the skill is the same: We must stop listening to fear and other self-defeating self-talk and replace it all with our true inner voice of courage. This is the

> **We must stop listening to fear and other self-defeating self-talk and replace it all with our true inner voice of courage.**

number one thing that separates people who succeed in achieving their dreams in life and those who don't. The courage to dream, and to live your dreams, often boils down to choosing the inner voice of courage over the other, self-defeating voices.

RECAP

- A lot of people work hard, but some paths can turn hard work into significant compensation, while many do not.

- Almost nothing can boost your courage more than working with a good mentor who has already succeeded in the things you want to pursue and achieve.

- Success demands that we learn to consistently replace all self-defeating self-talk with the voice of courage. It is extremely important to listen to the right voices.

- To really achieve our goals, it greatly helps to get our dreams bigger than our fears. If our fears are bigger, we usually let them run our lives. But if our dreams are bigger, this gives us a lot of energy and strength to overcome our fears and any other roadblocks to success—whatever they are.

- Reading books and listening to audios from people who have successfully overcome their fears and achieved their dreams is a great courage booster. We need daily doses of such material to help us continually win the inner battle between self-defeating self-talk and our inner courage.

- When you aim for success, a lot of people will try to talk you out of it. Some are simply justifying their own choices to remain average, and others sincerely think they're helping you if they can convince you to settle for less than your dreams. If you try to do big things, expect both kinds of opposition from some of the people around you.

- Instead of letting other people's criticisms and doubts join with your inner critic and increase your self-defeating thoughts, double down on pivoting all self-defeating voices immediately and directly to your voice of inner courage.

- While the voice of fear often spins out of control in your mind, exaggerating problems and ignoring positives, the voice of courage focuses on reality, solutions, and effective actions. The voice of courage is superior to the voice of fear.

- Moreover, the voice of fear usually lies, while the voice of courage faces reality head on and tells the truth. People who allow fearful voices to dominate their thinking usually struggle to succeed very much in life. While success is challenging even for people who listen to the voice of courage, it is much more likely because they focus on reality, solutions, taking action, and making good choices.

- Many people who haven't achieved great success struggle to see how important this inner battle really is. But successful people know that self-defeating self-talk holds them back, while the voice of courage greatly improves their lives. Winning this self-talk battle isn't the only thing needed to succeed, but it is an essential part of it.

CHAPTER 3

THE COURAGE TO LISTEN TO THE RIGHT VOICE

*"Courage is being scared to death...
and saddling up anyway."*
—John Wayne

To begin anything new takes courage. You are traveling into uncharted territory, beginning something without knowing the outcome. Initiative is required—and this is something we're seldom taught in today's schools or communities. In fact, most lessons tend to squelch innovation rather than promote and build it. Sometimes the beginning of a new business or project can be the scariest moment, the moment when courage matters most. This is the decision point.

It does not take much to look around and realize that most people are not pursuing their dreams. The average person watches approximately four hours of TV a day,[5] the home-based video and online game market is exploding with people playing games and immersing themselves in virtual realities. Recreational sports such as volleyball, basketball, darts, bowling, etc. seem to at be an all-time high.[6] Most of these are good things, for the most part, but they sometimes become distractions that keep us from doing something truly significant. It seems as if people are finding numerous ways to escape and just pass the time away. Of course, drinking and drug use have reached epidemic proportions in many communities.

People are often afraid to try to accomplish something significant. So many people want to "play it safe" with their work life (another way of standing with the bat on their shoulder instead of swinging at the ball)—and then use escapism in their personal life to cope. Well, I have some news for you: a lot of them aren't exactly thriving. My question to you is: Why play it safe? None of us is going to make it out of this life alive. We only get one shot at life, so why not really live it?

GOING AGAINST THE GRAIN

This reminds me of a quote by one of our mentors, Chris Brady: "There is no significance in a safe life, and no safety in a significant life." We learned very quickly that building a business means learning to take risk. In fact, really getting ahead requires some risk—but not the kind of escapist risk that makes "Must See TV" the highlight of our lives. People who are successful learn to risk in ways that actually help them get ahead in life, not just fall further into a lifetime rut of mediocrity or being average.

> It does not take much to look around and realize that most people are not pursuing their dreams.

Best-selling author Orrin Woodward once painted a very

vivid picture of what it takes to succeed. Imagine two lines at the airport or at a park celebration on a national holiday. In one line you find 300 people heading in one direction, and in the other line just one person lined up to go the other way.

This image just about captures success, leadership, and courage in a nutshell—in one easy-to-see snapshot. If your life is lived in the line with everyone else, you'll tend to get what the masses get—working hard just to make ends meet, depending on debt just to get by, and living paycheck to paycheck while your debt load and expenses grow.

From this illustration we can clearly see why success is so hard. Can you imagine the inner thoughts of the lone person going the other direction? When pretty much everyone around you is headed one way and you decide to go the opposite direction, you're naturally going to question if you're on the right path.

If I have learned anything from our success, it is that usually going against the crowd is the best approach. It takes courage to step out and go the other direction. As I said in an earlier chapter, not only will you face the inner thoughts of disbelief and question if you're doing the right things in such circumstances, many people will stop you along the way to point out that you are going the opposite direction.

I sometimes wonder how many people on their way to success turn back toward mediocrity based on the suggestion of the many. And if the suggestion of the many doesn't turn you around, the criticism may. It takes courage to go against the grain.

THE TEN PERCENT

Soon after starting our own business we were introduced to the book *Cashflow Quadrant* by Robert Kiyosaki. In this book the author explains that there are two very different ways to think about success. Around 90 percent of people believe that financial success is based on getting a job or a career working for someone else, and therefore they act a certain way while making a living and pursuing success. Only about 10 percent of people believe that entrepreneurship and business building is the path to financial success—and they behave accordingly. These aren't meant to be precise statistics, but they do illustrate the situation.

To be clear, the truth is a bit more detailed than this. Most people in the "90 percent" actually believe that business ownership brings more money, free time, and success, they just don't think that they personally can build a successful business that thrives. They think this is something that can only be done by a few people, like Steve Jobs or Bill Gates for example. "The rest of us," according to this viewpoint, "Will only get ahead with a good job or career," or "We'll never get ahead at all, so why try?" The inner voices of criticism reinforce this perspective in most people—to the point that they pass this self-defeating dialogue on to their children and anyone else who will listen.

Thus we end up with 300 or even 3,000 people in one line and only 1 person, or at most 2-3, in the other. Yes, most of the 300 know that nearly everyone in their line is living paycheck to paycheck and getting deeper into debt, but they are deathly afraid to join the other line. The voices of fear and doubt keep them from even trying to make a change.

> **I sometimes wonder how many people on their way to success turn back toward mediocrity based on the suggestion of the many. It takes courage to go against the grain.**

Of course, some people in the line of 1, 2, or 3 don't succeed either, and the voice of fear loudly warns almost everyone in the line of 300 about the dangers of the smaller line. Ironically, however, when a person in the shorter line does fail, his fallback position, his punishment if you will, is to rejoin the ranks of the longer line.

There is an even deeper reality in all this. I don't think the following survey has ever been officially taken in real life, since the two lines in this example are imaginary, but if you interviewed each person in both lines and found out who is thriving in life and living his or her dreams, I believe you'd discover a very interesting thing. I've done this kind of interviewing informally by speaking with many thousands of people over the years.

Nearly all people in the longer line typically give a lot of voice to self-doubt, self-criticism, and other self-defeating thoughts. On the other hand, the people in the smaller line are divided into two camps: those who also spend a lot of time listening to negative self-talk and only end up visiting the shorter line for a few months or years, versus those whose self-talk is almost exclusively the voice of courage and for the most part end up achieving great success.

Note that those focused on the voice of courage have to work hard to maintain this habit. It doesn't just happen for most people.

But the people in the lines who are truly succeeding nearly all have and keep developing the habit of putting aside self-defeating self-talk and focusing on the voice of courage. This is the big difference between the two lines. Also, find a person in the longer line who is following this habit and sticks to it, and it is almost always just a matter of time until he or she switches lines.

Courage isn't just a nice thing to have that helps you along in life; those who take most of their cues from their inner voice of courage tend to live very different lives than the majority of people. They live their dreams, because they listen to the right voice and take action based on what it tells them. Again, the masses, the "90 percent", so to speak, do not. Instead, the people in the longer line generally take most of their cues from self-defeating voices.

I KEPT SEEKING

I remember the seminar when this finally, really, hit home for me. It was late, I was exhausted, and I found myself doing everything I could to keep my eyes and mind open to catch even one nugget of information that would make a difference in my success. By this point we had read a lot of books and attended a number of seminars, soaking up wisdom from people who have learned to focus on the inner voice of courage and attained a lot of success in life.

I had learned a great deal from these studies, and it helped me in many different areas of my life. But I seemed to be missing something. I felt stuck and began to doubt that I was ever going to break through. After all, we had been building our business for several years, while working days in our regular jobs, and I felt tired. I wanted success to come more quickly, and more easily. But I hadn't fully changed my thinking yet—though I didn't know this at the time.

The speaker was about halfway through the talk when one of the most profound truths hit me. He stood on the stage and said something like this: "You need to stop listening to yourself, and start *talking* to yourself."

PRINCIPLE 10

CONFRONT THE INTERNAL VOICE

AT SOME POINT, WE MUST GO BEYOND LEVEL 1 THINKING (ALLOWING SELF-DFEEATING VOICES TO DOMINATE OUR THOUGHTS) AND LEVEL 2 THINKING (REPLACING ALL SELF-DEFEATING THOUGHTS WITH THE VOICES OF COURAGE); WE MUST REALLY ENGAGE LEVEL 3 THINKING: ACTIVELY LIVING ONLY BY THE VOICE OF COURAGE IN OUR DAILY LIVES.

(We need to actively make the voice of courage our consistent voice, day in and day out.)

As I processed this thought I began to worry: "Only crazy people talk to themselves, people who need help and should be hospitalized." Then it hit me: by having that very thought I was talking to myself! I did it all the time. We all do it. But, sadly, most of our self-talk is from the wrong fearful voices.

That night I realized just how much I talk to myself, and more importantly, how much I tended to listen and fear rather than actively speak. Most of my life I had listened mainly to self-defeating voices. Recently I had improved on this habit by beginning to listen to the voice of courage, and to put aside the voice of the inner-critic. It was a good start. But it wasn't enough.

I needed to fully engage the right voice. I needed to begin to *speak* with this voice, rather than just listen to it.

LIGHTENING STRIKE!

This created a major and sudden shift inside me.

I'm here to tell you that this jolt into reality can have an incredible impact on your daily life and attitude as well. Much of what we get done in life is based on the attitude we have about tasks at hand. When we strategize our year, or week, when we plan the specifics of our day or a given project, we can't let the voice of fear take over or undermine our efforts. But that's just a start. We also need to fully bring our voice of courage into everything we do. It needs to become our dominant voice.

> **We also need to fully bring our voice of courage into everything we do. It needs to become our dominant voice.**

In Orrin Woodward's bestselling book *Resolved: 13 Resolutions for Life* he explains:

"Inside a person's head are two voices. The first, the Positive Voice, speaks all the good about each situation, seeing the world through a positive perspective. The second, the Negative Voice, speaks all the bad about each situation, seeing the world from a negative perspective.

"One cannot eliminate the Negative or Positive Voice entirely, but one can learn to turn up and down each of them. Winners consistently turn up the Positive Voice and turn down the Negative Voice, leading to a healthy positive attitude on life. While others, those who struggle with their attitudes, reverse this process, turning up the negative Voice and turning down the Positive Voice.

"In fact, most people struggle with attitudes because they are wired with the Negative Voice shouting and the Positive Voice whispering at them."

KICK IT OUT OF THE WAY!

Sitting in my seat at the seminar, I found myself lost in an epiphany. I didn't hear another word the speaker shared. I began to realize that this whole time, I was my biggest obstacle. That's like a slap in the face!

But it's true. You are your biggest obstacle. If you listen to your inner critic (Level 1), you're blocking yourself from success and progress. If you learn to replace your inner critic with the voice of courage (Level 2), that's much better. But it's still not quite enough. The self-imposed roadblocks in your life are smaller at Level 2, but they're still holding you back in ways you probably don't quite grasp or understand.

LEVEL 1
Listening to your inner critic and other negative voices.

LEVEL 2
Replacing the voice of your inner critic with the voice of courage.

LEVEL 3
Building the habit of ONLY listening to the voice of courage, and ALWAYS listening to the voice of courage.

To really succeed, we need Level 3 thinking. We must progress from Level 1 to Level 2, and then we must go even further: we must learn to stop being bystanders in our own lives. We must go beyond merely watching our voice of fear and voice of courage argue with each other, and even beyond actively choosing the voice of courage instead of the voices of fear.

We must decide to consistently think and speak in the voice of courage. To make it our true voice. Our one voice.

The truth is, it really is our actual voice. The voices of fear are just imposters.

We must embrace the voice of courage. We must, every minute, every second of every day and night, make the voice of courage our voice. We must eat in this voice, drink in this voice, sleep and think and laugh and cry and live and love in this voice. It must *become* our voice. It already is our voice, deep down. But we must make it so in action. In every action.

We must embody this voice.

The inner voice of courage must become us. Or, more specifically, I realized:

The voice of courage must become me.

I must become the voice of courage.

I am the voice of courage.

I must become myself.

Not a divided, distracted, conflicted, weak version of me. I lived that version for far too many years. I must become the real me.

This occurs to the precise extent that I embrace the voice of courage. When I embrace my true voice, I am myself.

"This is who I am," I found myself thinking. I looked around and surprisingly found myself sitting in a large arena with thousands of other people. A speaker was sharing something from the stage. But the power of the transformation I was experiencing was so strong that I quickly transported again back into my thoughts.

My thinking had been the biggest obstacle in my life. I had begun to change my thinking, but I hadn't realized how far I needed to go. I couldn't be content with just playing referee—trying to keep the courageous voice a few points ahead of the inner critic. I needed to go all in, to immerse myself in the voice of courage. To become one with it.

It is my actual voice, after all. It is the real me. Why have I resisted just moving beyond the other voices and becoming me?

I had no answer. It didn't matter. I had more important things to think about: How do I become truly one with my voice of courage?

KICK IT ALL THE WAY GONE!

When I asked myself this question, another breakthrough came immediately. The voices of fear, self-doubt, and inner-criticism aren't part of me at all. They are foreign. Invaders. Attackers. Liars.

PRINCIPLE 11

THINK

THE VOICE OF FEAR, THE INNER-CRITIC, AND ALL OTHER SELF-DEFEATING VOICES AREN'T PART OF YOU, OR HELPFUL FRIENDS THAT JUST NEED TO BE KEPT IN CHECK; THEY ARE ENEMY VOICES.

(Know this. And treat them like it. Think about the voices in your mind. Have the courage to truly think in the voice of courage—the only real thinking.)

Something shifted inside me. I saw the truth for what it was, maybe for the first time in my life. "That's not me," I said. I knew it was true. The voices of fear and self-doubt looked dark and alien. "If they ever come back," I knew, "I won't call them My Inner Voices of Fear, Doubt, Inner-Critic, etc."

That's not who they really are. I know the truth now. "They are *the* Voices of Fear, Doubt, and Criticism. Not *my* voices. Not me. Just outside attacks. Enemies."

I was breathing rapidly at this point. The world around me disappeared, and I focused in on the power of this experience.

As we go through life, both good and bad things happen to us. We experience incredible highs and almost unbearable lows. And we live through many things between these extremes. We have situations where we feel like we cannot lose, and at other times all we do is lose. The same is true with winning.

These moments combine to create that inner voice that you hear throughout the day.

Here is what is so empowering: You chose that voice. You can live as a victim of your bad experiences. Or you can listen to the voice of the real you. You can simply *be* that voice. And it is the voice of courage.

The real you is the voice of courage. I shook my head in awe. *This is true. The real me is the voice of courage.*

The other voices, the defeating voices, are enemies, pure and simple. Not two sets of "your" inner voices. That's just not the truth. The reality is very different: your voice versus the enemy's voice. Courage versus fear.

You versus the enemy.

Period.

This is so important. It is worth repeating over and over until we really get it, until it becomes part of our understanding and view of the world:

Me = Courage
My Voice = Courage
Fear = The Enemy

I was taking notes as I experienced this breakthrough. I kept looking back at what I had written, then asking more questions. I was asking the voice of courage for answers, then speaking the answers in the voice of courage. I was actually taking charge of my own life. I was no longer dabbling with courage. I was fully immersed. I am courage.

PRINCIPLE 12

FIGHT THE REAL ENEMY

YOUR VOICE IS THE VOICE OF COURAGE.

**(Find yourself. Then be yourself. Always.
You are the voice of courage.
The voice of courage is you.
Immediately fight any other voice, and turn to the
voice of courage.)**

I took a deep breath and looked up at the speaker. But this time I saw through clear eyes, eyes that were now open. I saw a man who understood who he is. He spoke earnestly. He really cared about those of us in the audience. He wanted so badly to help us see, to help us grasp what we could become. Who we are.

I stared in awe.

I could see now what he was doing. Everything he said was meant to get us to embrace one thing: our true voice. The real me. All his stories, the examples, the diagrams, the quotes—trying to get me to stop fighting between enemy voices and my own and simply embrace my voice. The voice of courage.

Sometimes he spoke in a normal voice, other times he whispered—and occasionally he even yelled. But it all meant the same thing. Take the scales off your eyes and see. Take the plugs from your ears and hear. The inner-critic isn't actually "inner" because it's not you. It's your enemy. You are courage.

Stop listening to your enemy, and then go a step further: Stop engaging any battle between the enemy and courage. Just ignore the enemy altogether—it's not even worth your notice. Focus on you.

> **The inner-critic isn't actually "inner" because it's not you. It's your enemy. You are courage.**

On courage. And get to work on what courage wants you to do.

For the first time, I think, I actually heard what the speaker was teaching. Not the words, but the true essence of his message. He sat down, and another speaker was introduced. She taught the same message. The next speaker taught the same message again. I looked around in wonder. "I finally see what they are teaching."

I have never been the same since that experience.

I changed. Everything changed.

I sat in that chair and felt everything shift. Years of struggle and refusing to give up led to that moment. And when it came, the universe realigned. I felt it happen.

I looked up and smiled.

I know who I am.

RECAP

- The voices of self-doubt, self-criticism and fear aren't part of you. They are your enemies.

- The real you is the voice of courage.

- **Level 1** of the inner battle for success is listening to self-defeating voices, allowing fear and doubt to be the dominant voices in our minds.

- **Level 2** of the inner battle for success consists of consciously replacing all self-defeating voices with the voice of courage. This is an extremely important step.

- **Level 3** of the battle for success goes beyond Level 2 by actively engaging the voice of courage. It isn't enough to just fight the battle between the voices of fear and courage, we must take action to make courage the dominant voice in our everyday lives. We must begin speaking, thinking, and choosing in the voice of courage.

- Until you become one with the voice of courage, you will naturally undermine your own progress and success—often without even realizing it.

- You must be the voice of courage, and the voice of courage must be you. You have total power to make this happen—one thought at a time. You must learn to be all in, and entirely consistent in this choice. It must become a habit and the reality of your life.

- All successful people do this, either naturally or consciously. This is a vital and indispensible part of success. Those who don't do this don't achieve real success.

PART 2

COURAGE IN ACTION

*"If you're trying to achieve, there will be roadblocks.
I've had them; everybody has had them. But obstacles
don't have to stop you. If you run into a wall, don't turn
around and give up. Figure out how to climb it, go
through it, or work around it."*
—Michael Jordan

*"Never say never, because limits, like fears,
are often just an illusion."*
—Michael Jordan

CHAPTER 4

THE COURAGE TO TELL YOURSELF THE RIGHT STORY

"It's not what you say out of your mouth that determines your life, it's what you whisper to yourself that has the most power!"
—Robert Kiyosaki

When you know who you are, things change. To begin with, you know you're meant to succeed. You know you were born to do great things. You know it. Regardless of your past, you know that your future is meant to be lived in Technicolor: you are meant to be part of the "10 percent," not average. You'll *swing* at your dreams and opportunities from now on, because you know who you are.

Next, when this change comes, you suddenly realize that you have been following some very false scripts in your life. They don't apply to you—not the real you—but for some reason they have dominated your life. This happens because as we experience things in life, and then respond to these experiences using thinking dominated by the voices of fear and self-criticism, we start to believe falsehoods about who we are and where we are going in life. We can become very attached to these false paths in life. We often work very hard to keep ourselves following these storylines, even when they hurt us or hold us back.

For example, if you have a big goal or dream, and you know the things you need to do to achieve it, but you just can't seem to bring yourself to actually do the things that are needed, no matter how hard you try and no matter how much you seek motivation, there's a good chance your dream or goal is at odds somehow with an underlying storyline or script that you picked up somewhere along the way. Trying to move past such storylines, especially if we don't realize how they influence our daily actions, can be very difficult.

THE POWER OF SCRIPTS

Whenever I go out to speak and share how I used to be so shy and had no confidence, I have a line of people who come to me during the break and ask: "How did you overcome that?" I wish I had an easy way to tell them the answer, to show them how simple it really is. I try. But who can grasp it when they falsely believe the voices of fear and self-defeat? Or when they even believe that these voices are their own?

One of the most important and profound things I have ever learned in my life is that the storylines you tell yourself are powerful. They direct your life, your days, your minutes—even your thoughts and feelings. They often direct your actions, even when you don't realize this is happening. If you don't know your true story, you don't even know yourself. Not really.

For many years the story of me standing on the baseball diamond watching the pitches go past without swinging defined my life. But let's get real. The truth is that this experience only happened one time. It was over in five minutes. It isn't my life. It's just a short experience that happened many years ago.

However, I have replayed that failure and others like it thousands of times in my head. It was only one brief event in my life, but because I chose to internalize it as the story of my life, and feel its failure over and over again in my heart, it became the dominant voice in my world. It became my script. "Dan Hawkins is not a champion," this enemy voice consistently told me. "He is just an average guy who will only do average things."

Every time I was confronted with an opportunity, this was the voice that considered my options, made decisions, planned, and tried to improve. This story blocked me at every turn, usually without my conscious mind even realizing what was happening. I believed it was "my story," rather than merely "something I experienced or did." The difference is incredibly powerful.

> **We all have certain scripts and storylines etched into our minds, and if we believe them they create attitudes and patterns. The patterns then extend to all areas of life.**

We all have certain scripts etched into our minds, and if we believe them they create attitudes and patterns. The patterns then extend to all areas of life. For example, both my wife Lisa and I come from divorced families. All of the fighting and conflicts we watched and heard in our youth created an underlying storyline or script about marriage. That plot was colored mostly by bad experiences.

We both painted a clear mental picture that being married was a short-term situation and that when things went bad you just walk away. We believed that marriage is about selfishness and conditional love. I am not trying to use my parents' divorce as an excuse for my struggles or failures, but to say they had no impact on my marriage would be inaccurate.

I was in grade school when we were told that my parents were getting a divorce. I can remember the tension I felt as they explained what would happen. It went all the way in. So many emotions flooded my mind: anger, sadness, resentment, fear. Relational pain is some of the worst pain people can go through. The thought, "Did I cause this?" swirled in my mind.

It saddens me to see the divorce rate so high in America today.[7] The family unit is so important to a child's life. For me, the divorce was just the beginning of the pain that would come. On the one hand, some of the day-to-day fighting ended, but on the other hand a lot of things got much worse.

For example, as a young man I felt I had to choose which parent to love, whose side to take. Who to love and who to hate, even. Without even knowing it, I think, my parents tried to win our love by discrediting one another. It was kind of like a modern political race, less about a parent wanting to show us he or she cared about us and more about proving that the other person didn't care.

There was a secret place I used to go to get away and try to figure out what to do. It was down an abandoned railroad track, at a big oak tree with low hanging branches I could climb. I used to sit in the branches and just think. I remember the continuous tears and sadness. I felt myself being torn between wanting a dad who loved me and not hurting a mom whom I loved. We were given the chance to choose which parent we would live with, a choice no child should be forced to make. As I sat in the tree looking up to a blue sky, the sun sparkled through the leaves and bounced off the tears that rolled down my cheeks.

The story was written for me there, that day: Marriage causes pain, two people cannot be happy in marriage. Also, having children is a bad idea because the marriage will just end in divorce and I would never want my kids to bear this pain. That is the story I told myself over and over again. I carried it into my future relationships, and it subconsciously shaded every decision I made. I don't blame my parents or harbor any resentment. But this storyline had a major impact on my relationships.

I carried it into my future relationships, and it subconsciously shaded every decision I made.

SCRIPTING ALWAYS COMES OUT

Fast-forward many years. When Lisa and I first met it scared me half to death. To this point in my life I was living out my script of average "to a T". I had just finished tech school and was settling into an average job and life as an auto mechanic. I worked for the family business, because I was too afraid to interview for a different job. At this point, I had only been in two romantic relationships and the last one, with my fiancée (not Lisa), had just ended, exactly how I knew it would, based on the script of bad relationships the voices of fear had been telling me.

It was late one evening; I was in my early twenties and had just moved back home to live in my parents' basement. I only had a few of my personal belongings with me, and I needed to get the rest of my clothes. Earlier in the day I tried to reach out to my fiancée and asked if I could stop by our apartment and talk about our relationship. She said she was not going to be home that night because she was going out with friends and did not want to talk.

Knowing that she would be gone, I felt it would be a good time to run over and grab some of my clothes for the next week. As I drove I thought through the storyline of marriage I had etched in my mind. "See Dan, this is how it works. It doesn't. It always ends. Why even get married?" As I arrived at our low-income apartment I was sure I should end the relationship but I was too afraid to be alone. I had such low self worth that I told myself: "Even though I am not happy with her, I won't be able to find anyone else."

As I walked up the stairs to the second floor I was torn between two conflicting storylines. One voice kept saying, "Leave. Marriages don't work anyway, just stay single and have fun." The other voice told me: "I know you aren't happy, but look at you, who else would want to be with you?"

Actually, my script against marriage and relationship happiness was so deep that I didn't even realize that both of these voices came from fear and doubt. Sometimes we think our inner self-talk is between fear and courage, when in fact our inner critic is playing both sides of the battle. It pretends to be the voice of courage when it says things like: "Leave this relationship." But it follows up with words that only come from the voice of fear: "Marriage never works. Why try?"

This kind of ganging up on us naturally happens if we let self-defeating voices dominate our thoughts.

PRINCIPLE 13

TELL A NEW STORY

THE VOICES WE LISTEN TO CREATE MOMENTUM, EITHER FOR FEAR AND NEGATIVES, OR FOR COURAGE AND ACTION. OVER TIME THEY CREATE A STORYLINE OR SCRIPT IN OUR LIVES.

(If we let an enemy voice dominate, it will join up with other hurtful voices and gang up on us, strengthening the wrong plots and storylines in our daily experience.)

THE VOICE OF DESPAIR

I knew my fiancée and I were having problems, but this all become worse when I walked into our apartment and found her in a romantic setting with a guy we knew from college. It's hard for me to express my feelings, even years later. This took me right to the edge of pure misery. I felt so betrayed, so hurt, so rejected. I felt deeply alone.

I lost my temper, and started shouting at her and the man she was with. The arguing was loud, and some of the neighbors called the police. Someone pulled the guy and I away from each other before it became a full-blown physical fight, and I found myself sitting on the stairs in as much pain as I've ever felt.

Our months of dysfunction, and then our argument and breakup seemed to verify the script I had been telling myself for years about my lack of self-worth. As I said, the voices of fear really like to combine negative scripting, gang up on us, and hit us with a double blow or triple blow; in this case, both my script of "low self-worth" and the script of "all relationships end badly" played in my mind simultaneously. I felt a deep despair, and I could hardly breathe.

I thought about how bad I must be that I could not make her happy, and now it was over. I remember resting my forehead on my clinched fists and saying a prayer with tears streaming down my face. "Lord, please help me understand this. What am I going to do?"

As I sat on the stairs trembling, fists clinched, tears running down my face, I wanted someone to pay for this pain. I wanted someone to pay for this pain. Fear kicked in as I realized I was going to be alone, and I began telling myself over and over that I was not good enough.

As I sat alone in overwhelming pain, one of the police officers sat down next to me on the stairs and asked what had happened. As I explained what took place, something incredible transpired. I don't even remember the name of this officer but I do remember what he said. "You seem like a good guy with a good head on your shoulders. Walk away and do something with your life."

I am not sure if he realized the impact he had on me that night. I was trapped by my low self-image and stories I had been telling myself. The scripts had caught me in their web. He, maybe without even knowing it, started me on the path to changing my story. He helped me realize that my low self-image is what led to this, and this wasn't who I actually am. It took something painful to wake me up, to help me realize that I was in control, that I could walk away and do something with my life.

Moments like these can either define us or refine us.

The difference comes in the story you tell yourself about your life and experiences. Again, our storylines

Moments like these can either define us or refine us.

are incredibly powerful. They are basically the voices of fear and self-criticism, or the voice of courage, after they've taken root and are deep down in our hearts. They become our subconscious direction, our "elephant". And once they have momentum, they take us in a certain direction—even if we don't realize what is happening.

This goes beyond fighting to keep our positive voice winning against our negative voice. As long as these two sides are in battle, the deeper storylines of our life keep going in the same direction as our dominant momentum. We have to get to Level 3 thinking, where we simply stop giving any energy to the voices of fear and submit entirely to the voice of courage.

When I finally realized that the voices of fear are the enemy, and that the voice of courage is me, I started submitting to courage. I just gave in and went with courage. I still had to replace the voices of fear with the voice of courage at times, because I had bad habits of listening to self-defeating voices. But I now knew the truth: voices of fear are the enemy. I am the voice of courage.

Always sticking with the voice of courage made a huge difference. But I still had to deal with the false storylines I had picked up over the years. I had to confront the script of "I am only average", and the script of "marriage is always bad". Both were lies. Both were from enemy voices. I had to learn to replace such scripts with the voice of courage.

I was born for greatness. That's my true story. That's my real script. And it's yours too. Marriage to Lisa has been the greatest joy of my life, and without the breakup from my earlier fiancée, this would never have happened. Today Lisa and I have five beautiful daughters that make life worth living. Voices that depart from these truths are enemies. If they ever come up, even a little bit, I know I have to immediately replace them with my voice. The voice of courage.

When we find ourselves being held back or blocked from what we know we should do, it is powerful to identify what scripts and habits we are allowing to remain in our way. For example, it wasn't until I realized that my boyhood fear of swinging my bat in the big game had become a life path, and that it was recurring in other parts of my life, that I could address it and replace it with the voice of courage. Once I did this hard work of inner change, I began to think, choose, and act differently.

PRINCIPLE 14

CREATE NEW HABITS

WE MUST ENGAGE LEVEL 4 THINKING: NOTICING WHEN WE COME UP AGAINST ROADBLOCKS IN LIFE, SEARCHING AND FINDING WHAT FALSE STORYLINES ARE HOLDING US BACK, AND ALWAYS REPLACING SUCH STORYLINES WITH THE VOICE OF COURAGE.

(False storylines about our life can be buried so deeply inside us that they influence us even when we don't realize it. When we just can't bring ourselves to change, even when we want to and even when we know what we need to do, we are often being held back by false storylines and scripts. This is the time to engage Level 4 thinking. We must call the false storylines what they are (lies), and keep our minds focused on the true storyline and the right habits—from the voice of courage.)

Sometimes the scripts we find inside us are surprising. One of our mentors, Orrin Woodward, found himself held back from the success he wanted until he faced his roadblocks and realized that an experience from his youth was causing him to avoid the voice of courage. This stemmed from a dance he was invited to attend in the awkward years just before high school. Part of the theme of the dance was to dress up in a costume (the dance cost $2 without a costume, only $1 for those who came in costume), but young Orrin didn't have a ready-made costume so he asked his mother for help.

They came up with a cute bumblebee costume, replete with a cape and little homemade tail/stinger. When Orrin arrived at the event, however, none of the other kids were dressed up in costume. To make matters worse, they reacted to his costume in a way he hadn't expected. They laughed and laughed. The pointed fingers, derision, and group scorn broke the little boy's heart. He had to escape and call home for a ride to rescue him.

Later in life, Orrin found himself avoiding important actions that were needed for success in his work—because his inner self worked very hard to avoid being laughed at for any reason. To take some of the risks that would make his goals a reality, he needed to ignore the laughter or scorn of others and boldly do what was needed. But he couldn't bring himself to do this until he confronted this powerful script from his youth.

For a moment, put yourself in his shoes—as a little boy going to one of his first dances and wanting badly to fit in, only to be laughed at and mocked. Then vowing never again to put yourself in a position to be mocked by others. Then finding that to succeed in your business goals you need to be fine facing laughter and derision from others, and going forward with boldness regardless of what people might think.

The only way past this is to consistently replace every thought that holds you back with the voice of courage. This can and should become a habit, but at first it requires you to consciously make this shift in your mind and heart every time the potential of being laughed at arises. Such powerful change—every time the worry and fear comes up, over and over—is a necessary part of achieving success. Find a truly successful person, in any field or walk of life, and you'll find someone who has gone through this kind of shift.

Or consider the story of Kevin.[8] He started a business with his wife and desperately wanted to succeed. In fact, he worked very hard to reach his goals, only to find that he simply couldn't bring himself to make the nightly calls that were needed to succeed in his sales business. At his day job, he was a respected part of the team, but when it came time for he and his wife to get on the phone and call respective buyers, he froze up. He always met the minimum number of calls suggested by his mentor, but it was very hard for him. Once he met with the people, he found it almost impossible to go off script and respond naturally to their thoughts and questions.

Instead, he focused on the script the company gave him, and quickly steered any questions from the clients back to the script. Needless to say, few people bought anything from him. His wife picked up some of the slack, easily making friends with clients and addressing their needs, but Kevin even messed this up by interrupting and going back to the prepared sales script. His mentors tried to get him to change this, but he couldn't bring himself to change.

When he learned about Level 4 thinking, Kevin faced his life and asked himself why he allowed this problem to keep blocking him from his goals. As he considered this, he remembered an experience from his childhood. One day he had taken his crayons and colored markers out with the goal of drawing something very interesting to him. Like many budding artists, he wasn't sure what to draw until he got started, but he knew he passionately wanted to paint a masterpiece—or what passes for a masterpiece in the mind of a young boy with a handful of markers.

At first he worked on large, blank sheet of art paper. But this just didn't seem good enough somehow, so he went looking for a better place to express his art. He found a perfect canvas right in his home, the beautiful wall in the family living room. He sat next to the wall, arranged his markers and crayons so he could pick any color he wanted to as needed, and he began drawing his passion. When he was finished, he was excited to show members of his family what he had created.

The result wasn't at all what he had expected. Instead of praise and accolades, he was met with anger and punishments. The worst came from his father, who yelled at him, asked him what he was thinking, and why he would do such a thing, and then yelled even louder while grounding him and making him clean up the "mess." With cleanser and rags in hand, tears running down his face, he painfully adopted an inner script of never "coloring outside the lines again," of always "staying on the prescribed path," "always doing exactly what others want," "never venturing into the realm of creativity."

This stayed with him, burned into his heart and mind by the pain of the experience. Years later, in meeting after meeting, Kevin found that he simply couldn't relax, get to know people, and spend time off script just talking to them. His mentors and wife told him that this was necessary for his success, but he just couldn't bring himself to do it. Whenever they were "off script" in a meeting, he found himself sweating, his hands got clammy, and he anxiously pushed back to the prepared outline for the sales script. Never mind that even the official script suggested taking time to make friends and answer questions; Kevin only felt comfortable when he was saying what the script said, rote and memorized.

When he realized that his inability to relax, connect with others, and sell effectively was at odds with this boyhood experience, he adamantly told his mentors that he couldn't change. "I have to stay on script, stay within the lines," he told them. "I can't wing it. I just can't."

Even after hours of training and many attempts to redirect this painful storyline, Kevin refused to make the change. He reached the point where he never called anyone to set up sales meetings, and when he was honest with himself and others he admitted that it was extremely stressful because he knew such calls might end up with him in a meeting focusing on the script while the clients wanted to talk about other things. He needed to replace all such thoughts and habits with the voice of courage, but he choose not to. He eventually stopped building a business and focused on work where he could stay on a prepared script and not have to improvise—even in little ways. He didn't let the voice of courage heal him.

People who achieve success in life learn to adopt Level 4. They face false past storylines and replace them with the voice of courage. This habit allows them to build other habits that lead to success. Without this kind of inner change, success is always elusive.

LEVEL 1

Listening to your inner critic and other negative voices.

LEVEL 2

Replacing the voice of your inner critic with the voice of courage.

LEVEL 3

ONLY listening to the voice of courage, and ALWAYS listening to the voice of courage.

LEVEL 4

Searching out false storylines in our lives and replacing them with the voice of courage. Winners don't make the rules in the game of life.

TRUE STORYLINES

Sometimes it takes struggle to face our false scripting and choose Level 4. For me, after the painful breakup with my fiancée, that one statement from the officer helped me tell a new story about my life. What I thought was ruining my life was actually setting me free to live the life I truly wanted. I wish I could say the hurt was magically gone with this realization, but it wasn't. It took a little time to get past the feelings of what happened, but I knew I was on the right path.

Earlier I said that when I met Lisa it scared me. Here is what this means. In movies people frequently fall in love, and sometimes they even experience love at first sight. I do not know if that's exactly what happened for Lisa, but I know it happened for me. I realize this is cliché, but it's true: There was a moment after we met where it seemed like time stood still.

Lisa jumped into the front passenger seat of the vehicle. Her sister pointed back at me and said, "This is Dan, and it's his birthday today." Lisa looked back and said, "Hello. Happy birthday." I looked at her and smiled. It seemed like we looked at each other forever, and I got the feeling that we would someday be together. Like I said, it was love at first sight.

Of course, I was too chicken to tell anybody, but as she walked away after the drive I knew I would see her again. Then my subconscious failure storyline kicked in and I thought to myself, "She would never give you the time of day! Who are you fooling?"

Over a year passed before we saw each other again. During that time my fiancée and I broke up, and the police officer told me I could get my life together and do something important. God works in mysterious ways.

I was invited to my friend Chris's birthday party, and she told me that her sister Lisa was going to take us out for the evening. The first stop was a Mexican restaurant where a bunch of us met to eat dinner before the night began. Fate seated me right next to Lisa. I remember thinking many times that night how incredible she was, beautiful, smart, fun, and kind. I also remember thinking, "You do not stand a chance, Dan!" The false storylines are persistent.

We didn't say much during the evening, but I think both of us felt a connection. The next night Chris had a birthday party at her house and Lisa was there as well. This night was different, less awkward, and from the beginning of the party we relaxed and talked. We were amazed at all the things we had in common.

I was having the night of my life, and then the old voices came. My false scripting just chimed in every chance it got:

"She is just being nice because I'm her sister's friend."
"Come on Dan, really. You think she would date a guy like you?"
"I've got no chance with her."

Then it happened. At the end of the night she handed me a piece of paper with her name and number and asked me to call her tomorrow night between 6-9. "Is this some kind of sick joke?" my scripting asked me. Or did she really see something in me?

The next night could not come soon enough. I watched the clock all day as if it were moving in slow motion. Finally the moment of truth, time to make the call. I picked up the phone and began to dial her number. I kept getting so close and then slamming down the phone. My past scripting was running the show now.

Questions raced through my mind:

"Does she really like me? How could she?"

"What will I say? I never know what to say."

"Is this even her real phone number? I will probably call and someone will answer 'Kentucky Fried Chicken, how can I help you?'"

These are literally the thoughts I had as I struggled with the phone. After 2½ hours of this I was so frustrated. This is what it feels like when what we want collides with an underlying false script. We know what to do, but we just can't quite seem to make ourselves do it.

The solution? We must let the voice of courage win. We have to just do the thing we know we should. It helps to directly deal with our false storyline. In fact, this is essential if we want to truly overcome the problem.

I struggled as the 9 o'clock deadline to call her approached. The inner voice of courage began to quietly speak. *What if she actually does like you? What if you call and it goes well?*

Drawing from that faint seed of courage, I hit the last digit and refused to hang up again. The phone began to ring. We talked for hours that night, and we haven't missed a night talking now in over 16 years. The script was wrong. Enemy. Bad. Thank goodness I stepped up and let the voice of courage lead.

We have had many struggles in our marriage, of course. It hasn't been perfect by any means. The "Divorce" word was tossed around way too many times to count. After our first child we almost decided to stop having kids because of fear. So many times I almost gave in to those old false storylines about who I was and the idea that marriage always fails.

> **I had to rewrite the false storyline about marriage in order to have a great relationship with my wife and kids today.**

I had to rewrite the false storyline about marriage in order to have a great relationship with my wife and kids today. I look around at my family now and it is so different than the story that was being written. We seem to have a better marriage by the day, and we have five beautiful daughters who, God willing, will have a better storyline to start with.

All of us have false scripting in life. My purpose in sharing these experiences isn't to say "poor me" but rather to affirm that false storylines can be rewritten. You have the power to rewrite any story.

I am blessed that my parents chose to rewrite their false storylines as well, to learn from mistakes and start anew. I have watched them both move past the bitterness and repair relationships with us and to a certain extent with each other.

In fact, my dad began living his dreams again when he started in business with us. He was one of my first business partners, and we have worked together now for over thirteen years—and have seen a lot of success together. It's great to see the spark back in his eyes.

The truth is that all of us are in control of our thoughts and need to take responsibility to write the correct story.

BUT HOW?

So how do we do it? The first thing is to understand how our minds work. One of the best illustrations of this can be found in *The Magic of Thinking Big* by David Schwartz. As he put it so eloquently:

> "Your mind is a 'thought factory.' It's a busy factory, producing countless thoughts in one day. Production in your thought factory is under the charge of two foremen, one of whom we will call Mr. Triumph and the other Mr. Defeat. Mr. Triumph is in charge of manufacturing positive thoughts. He specializes in producing reasons why you can, why you're qualified, why you will. The other foreman, Mr. Defeat, produces negative, depreciating thoughts. He is your expert in developing reasons why you can't, why you're weak, why you're inadequate. His specialty is the 'why-you-will-fail' chain of thoughts.

"Both Mr. Triumph and Mr. Defeat are intensely obedient. They snap to attention immediately. All you need to do to signal either foreman is to give the slightest mental beck-and-call. If the signal is positive, Mr. Triumph will step forward and go to work. Likewise, a negative signal brings Mr. Defeat forward.

"To see how these two foremen work for you, try this example. Tell yourself, 'Today is a lousy day.' This signals Mr. Defeat into action and he manufactures some facts to prove you are right. He suggests to you that it's too hot or it's too cold, business will be bad today, sales will drop, other people will be on edge, you may get sick, your wife will be in a fussy mood. Mr. Defeat is tremendously efficient. In just a few moments he's got you sold. It is a bad day. Before you know it, it is a heck of a bad day.

"But tell yourself, 'Today is a fine day,' and Mr. Triumph is signaled forward to act. He tells you, 'This is a wonderful day. The weather is refreshing. It's good to be alive. Today you can catch up on some of your work.' And then it is a good day.

"In like fashion Mr. Defeat can show you why you can't sell [to] Mr. Smith; Mr. Triumph will show you that you can. Mr. Defeat will convince you that you will fail while Mr. Triumph will demonstrate why you will succeed. Mr. Defeat will prepare a brilliant case against Tom while Mr. Triumph will show you more reasons why you like Tom.

"Now the more work you give either of these two foremen, the stronger he becomes. If Mr. Defeat is given more work to do, he adds personnel and takes up more space in our mind. Eventually, he will take over the entire thought-manufacturing division, and virtually all thought will be of a negative nature. [At this point, he has the momentum of an elephant versus an ant, as discussed above.]

"The only wise thing to do is fire Mr. Defeat. You don't need him. You don't want him around telling you that you can't, you're not up to it, you'll fail, and so on. Mr. Defeat won't help you get where you want to go, so boot him out.

"Use Mr. Triumph 100 percent of the time. When any thought enters your mind, ask Mr. Triumph to go to work for you. He'll show you how you can succeed."

For many years Mr. Defeat was writing my story. The results were clear: fear and struggle, and very little success.

> **We need to take control of our thought life and write an empowering story.**

We need to take control of our thought life and write an empowering story. This is a process that requires constant awareness of your thoughts.

Once I realized how much I talk to myself I took a little time to listen. Now, I encourage you: do not spend too much time here listening to negative thoughts. Just do it enough to understand what your dominant thoughts are right now.

Orrin Woodward calls the thoughts that are holding us back limiting beliefs. If you are going to overcome a limiting belief the first step is to identify it. Orrin has shared that during his mentoring sessions he spends a lot of time listening to how people talk, what they say and how they think. Through this process he is able to begin identifying their limiting belief and help them develop a plan to over come it. Similarly, you can do this with your own self-talk by listening to what you say to yourself.

And when you run up against roadblocks that you just can't seem to overcome, it might be more than your normal self-talk that is the problem. It could be that you have a deep, underlying false storyline and script working against you. If you just can't bring yourself to do what you know you should, or need to, in order to meet your goals, search for false storylines that could be blocking your progress.

When you find such scripting in your mind, engage Level 4 thinking: replace any and every thought that supports the false storyline with your inner voice of courage. Focus on the real storyline. This is vital. All successful people learn to do this. People who don't do it, either naturally or consciously, simply don't achieve true success. It's that real. And that powerful.

Keep yourself constantly focused on thoughts that support your true storyline. Replace any distraction, anything that aligns with false storylines, immediately with the voice of courage. Make this a conscious habit, so that it can eventually develop into a subconscious habit. Always keep your thoughts on the true storyline. Always.

BEYOND IMPORTANT

This might seem like a little thing, but it isn't. It is the biggest thing you can do to ensure success in your life. Successful people do this; unsuccessful people don't.

This is real. It is a major difference between the 300 and the 1, or the "90 percent" and the "10 percent".

Your mind is like a garden of thoughts. Imagine a flower or garden box filled with new, rich black soil. Nothing is in the box but dirt. This is like our minds before we have any experiences or inputs. If you have spent any time around gardens, you know one thing for certain: If you leave the dirt alone it will not stay just dirt, weeds will grow.

This might seem like a little thing, but it isn't. It is the biggest thing you can do to ensure success in your life.

Think about that. It amazes me that no one has to plant weeds, there is not an elaborate plan and a ton of work that goes into growing a weed garden. It just happens. Our minds do the same thing: our natural tendency is to grow negative thoughts. Why? Because enemy thoughts are always at work. If we are not careful, negative "weeds" will take over our thinking and damage or undermine everything we do. This is the natural situation for almost everyone.

While we were serving for my church a few years ago, we got involved in a program called Faith Works. It was a service project where a group of volunteers went into the community and helped people with things they couldn't financially or physically do themselves. On one occasion we were at the home of a lady who was too ill to manage her flower garden any longer. On the form that she filled out for Faith Works she requested that we pull the weeds and leave the flowers.

Here is where it got interesting. We sat for a good half hour and stared at the flowerbed, debating what was a weed and what was a flower. We didn't realize it at the time, but at some point during the conversation she walked to the window above and overheard us. It did not take long at all before she hurried out and requested we leave the flowerbed alone. If we couldn't identify the weeds from the flowers, we would ruin her garden. Better not to touch it.

This begs a great question: How do I know the flowers from the weeds? This is where I began to realize how powerful the information I put in my mind and the people I associated with really were. I once heard a speaker sum it up very well: "If you want better results in your life stop taking your own advice." If we listen to our old, wrong voices, we won't get better results. We have to change.

We all make the best choices based on the information we have. So if we are making bad or mediocre choices, pulling out flowers instead of weeds, maybe it is time to get better information. To listen to the voices of people who have actually achieved the kinds of things we truly want.

As we listen to and read the words of such people, we begin to learn the difference between the flowers and the weeds. We usually don't know this all on our own. The best way to get the proper thinking is to give ourselves a constant diet of "right" thinking. A very effective way to do this is to make it a habit to listen to 2-3 audios a day, from people who have already succeeded, and read at least 15 minutes from a good book. Also, it is important to find as many opportunities as possible to hang out with people who are very successful.

Finding and working with a mentor at this point is key. When you have a trusted mentor, someone with your best interests in mind, he or she can help you identify your bad thinking (weeds). He calls out blind spots and other areas in your life that are hurting you. By definition, if they are blind spots you may never see them. A mentor can speak truth with love into your life. He can help you identify the blind spots (weeds) and point you in the right direction to focus on the right thinking (flowers) in your mind.

Once you have a good mentor, it is very important to really listen and to follow his advice. I have seen many people argue with their mentor, trying to hold on to the things that haven't worked for them in the past. Remember, as I once heard a great speaker and author say, if you argue for your limitations you get to keep them.

The job of a good mentor is to help you get to the root of your bad thinking—the things that are holding you back. If you were already doing the right things, or did not have a problem, you would not be stuck where you are. This is where "the speed of trust" comes in, as Stephen Covey taught. You need to trust your mentor and realize that if your mentor only tells you things you already know and are already doing, you wouldn't feel the need to change very much.

This lesson applies when it's time to go about changing or rewriting our false storylines, including any story that follows the voice of our fears rather than our courage. In short, we need to notice when false scripting is at work. This isn't always easy. Most people spend much of their life not realizing that these scripts are influencing their actions.

To overcome this natural weakness, we need to get our courage receptors up and running. We need to know clearly whenever the voices of fear (weeds) start whispering in our ear, and to pivot our thinking to the voice of courage (flowers). This must be learned.

Again: we need to learn to notice the difference between voices, and the best way to do this is to listen to and associate with people who already have this skill and habit.

UPGRADE YOUR DAILY LEVELS OF NATURAL COURAGE

What can we do? To begin with, we must keep our daily levels of natural courage as high as we can. It helps to start by feeding yourself a daily dose of positive information. For example, I begin my days with Bible study and prayer. I have found over the years that starting this way gets my mind in the right place. It sends me off for the day focusing on the right principles and thankful for who am I and what I have. Starting and ending each day with thoughts of thankfulness can really change your attitude.

Next, each day I try to jump into a good book or listen to quality audios that are aimed at self-improvement. I believe it is crucial to wisely feed your mind, body and soul on a daily basis. This will help support your foundations of courage so you can effectively tend your garden and notice when fear-based scripting starts to grow in your life.

PRINCIPLE 15

PERSEVERE

SUPPORT THE VOICE OF COURAGE BY PERSISTENTLY DOING THE LITTLE THINGS EACH DAY THAT UPGRADE YOUR NATURAL LEVELS OF COURAGE.

(This can include prayer, reading scripture, meditation, reading your list of goals every morning and every night, posting powerful quotes or moving pictures on your mirror, desk, or the screen of your phone, etc. Make a routine that boosts your basic level of courage, and follow it every day. Keep doing this, always.)

Likewise, in caring for a garden daily work is needed to identify and pull weeds before they overrun the flowers, vegetables, or whatever you want to grow. Your mind and thoughts are exactly the same.

As Ralph Waldo Emerson put it: "Belief consists in accepting the affirmations of the soul; unbelief, in denying them." Emerson is right on! And it is interesting that the following phrases are so similar:

> He has soul!
> He has courage!
> He has heart!
> He has spirit!

According the *Oxford English Dictionary* the word "soul" comes from Germanic roots and emphasizes the eternal or most core part of a person.[9] It is our true self. It is the lasting, real us. I also find it interesting that the words "courage" and "heart" actually come from the same root: "from Old French *corage*…", meaning 'heart, innermost…'", based on the Latin "*cor*", which is the word for "heart."[10]

Core, heart, and courage are the same word, ultimately, and they mean the same thing as spirit and soul: the innermost part of us, the true self, the courageous self. Indeed, the phrase "take heart" means to "take courage", the word "spirited" means "actively courageous,"[11] the same as the Latin phrase *carpe diem*, which means: "seize the day!"

The voice of courage is the true voice of the soul. When we have real soul, we are listening to the voice of courage. When we have spirit, we courageously take action. But when we lack soul, we lack courage—and heart.

The path to success is the path of learning to always put the voice of courage above any enemy voices like fear, self-doubt, and the inner critic. And if something is holding us back, we need the voice of courage to search out the root cause, and replace it with the right voice.

It really is this simple. It's not always easy, for sure, because changing our thoughts for the long-term is perhaps the hardest thing about success.[12] But it is simple. The key is to simply do it, and keep doing it. Persistance and perserverance, whatever happens, are so important. They are essential to success.

For example, I was driving late one night, headed 4 hours north of my home after an already long day at work. I had a lead on a customer that might be interested, and I was working very hard, trying to launch my company so I could be free from the 9-5 grind. This night came on the heels of one of the worst losing streaks I have ever experienced. I had 15 appointments over thirty days and every one of them ended with the dreaded words: "No, it's just not for us." It felt like striking out fifteen times in a row.

While I was driving that night I received a voice message from my mentor. He forwarded a note he had received from one of the business owners I was trying to help. It went something like this:

"Hey, Eric, this is ..... I just wanted your advice. We are working directly with Dan on this project but I'm not sure if he can give us what we need. We love him and all but... well...he just isn't getting the results we want. We believe he is slowing us down, and if we could work with you directly instead of him, we would be much more successful."

I was floored. Now to be fair, my mentor sent me this message to encourage me—excited that this couple was motivated to achieve results. That isn't exactly how I took it.

For me this message just reassured my voice of fear that I was not a good leader. The inner voice of courage was suffocated by the inner critic, screaming: "You don't have what it takes!" This was a true low spot for me. As the inner critic began to drag up so many examples of why I would fail, and as I listened instead of replacing these thoughts with the voice of courage, I got more and more discouraged.

I considered just turning my car around, cancelling my appointment that night, and calling it quits. I tried to respond to my mentor with a brave voice: "Hey Eric, thanks for the message. I, I,

I......" I did this several times, but when I began to break up and cry, I just ended each call. I must of tried to send 6 messages—all ended in me crying.

About 5 minutes later, while I was still headed to my appointment but contemplating turning around, my phone rang. It was my mentor Eric. Quickly I tried to compose myself, wiping my eyes and clearing my throat. "Hey Eric, how's it going?" I asked, trying to hide my despair. "Great," he responded. "I was just calling because the last six messages I received from you all ended with you upset and hanging up."

That was when I first realized that if you don't hit send (in that particular messaging system), the messages still get sent! Now I felt even worse.

I broke down and shared my frustration with Eric. I don't remember exactly what he said that night. But I do know he helped me understand that any great endeavor has its struggles. The ones who make it are usually the ones who just hang on while others are shaken off by the turbulence.

I began to realize that I had a choice: Buy into my excuses and quit, or double down. I thought about it as I drove, and I finally refocused on the voice of courage, decided to learn from the last month of failures, and chose to stay strong and win. I kept swinging!

I did make the appointment that night, or at least I showed up. But, true to the rut I was in, the prospective customer never came. I put in another success audio and began my four-hour drive home in the late night and early morning hours.

I kept focused on the voice of courage as I drove. "Every successful person had struggles, and had to persist in the face of whatever storms made their work difficult." I not only heard these words in my mind, I knew they were true. "You are writing your story, Dan," I told myself. "What kind of story would it be if you didn't face resistance. If you didn't have to struggle and look quitting right in the face and make a conscious and difficult decision to persist?"

I wish I could say everything got easier and totally changed from that point on. The truth is that I got to 31 "no's" before I got the next "yes". But that didn't matter, because I had already decided. The voice of courage was my focus. I would rather get a thousand "no's" than give up. Such decisions take soul, heart, and courage, but they are the path to success.

EXERCISE

- Is there anything in your life that you know you need to do, that would help you achieve your goals, but you just can't seem to bring yourself to do it? If so, you may be dealing with an underlying script or storyline that is buried in your subconscious.

- Try writing down the thing you know you need to do, and then brainstorm anything that might be holding you back. Spend some real time and effort on this. Find anything that is blocking your success, keeping you from doing what you need to do.

- Make this as simple as possible. Just ask: What is holding me back from X (the thing I know I should be doing, but can't seem to ever do)? What limiting beliefs are holding me back from X? What life experiences are holding me back from X? What failures or bad things in my life are holding me back from X? What is making me afraid or unable to do X? Keep asking such questions until you figure out what underlying storylines, if any, are blocking your success.

- Once you find a blockage, use the voice of courage to listen, learn, and then rescript the storyline. Afterward, always replace thoughts of the false storyline with the voice of courage.

- Repeat this exercise any time you find yourself unable to just set a goal and then do it. Find whatever is holding you back, and kick it out of your way. This is frequently a limiting belief or false script that you've accepted at some point in your life.

- This kind of personal internal work is a vital part of achieving success. This is one of the main reasons elite athletes frequently hire personal coaches to get them past underlying roadblocks. Find any roadblocks and figure out how to overcome them. If the roadblocks are based on false storylines, the way to overcome them is to rewrite the false scripting—by fully submitting to the true storyline and the voice of courage, and giving no thought or energy to anything that supports false scripting. Go all in to the new, true, storyline, 100 percent.

- You'll know you've been successful in this process when you begin replacing every negative thought tied to your false storyline with the voice of courage, and when you are now able to do the thing(s) you know you need to do in order to succeed.

- This is one of the most important exercises you will ever do in your life. Do it as often as needed. Successful people do this or some form of it to get past roadblocks; unsuccessful people do not.

CHAPTER 5

THE COURAGE TO CONFRONT

"If you want to live the life you have always wanted, you need to address the things you have always avoided."
—Orrin Woodward

We were attending the highest-level meeting for which we had ever qualified. It was a long weekend packed with so many great and challenging messages. My wife and I attended this seminar together, excited to take our company to the next level and do something big.

Speaker after speaker took the stage and seemed to speak right at us. You know the feeling: it was as if someone knew all our specific struggles and handed each speaker a note as they went on stage that explained what we needed. This was by far the most challenging workshop we had ever attended to date.

We were so enthused with everything we were learning, but by Saturday afternoon we started experiencing a sense of overload. We had so much to work on, so many things to change, and the thought of adding to our growing list of things to do began feeling a bit overwhelming.

The last day of the event, a Sunday, Lisa and I both woke up both on edge and mentally stressed to the max. As we began to get ready for the day, Lisa started hinting that we should leave early to get back to the kids. As the morning progressed, the hinting slowly changed to demands.

I kept taking notes as I listened to the presenters, but by this point I was tired and frazzled. I kept looking forward to the keynote event, the last speaker of the weekend. I hoped his message would help me calm down and get some sense of how to prioritize and effectively implement everything I knew I needed to change.

A break came, and when we went into the hall to stretch we started arguing about whether we should stay or go. I wanted to stay and hear the last talk, but Lisa was dead set on leaving. Like most fights in our marriage at that time, Lisa won. I walked, or maybe more honestly I stomped into the conference room, tapped my dad on the shoulder and said, "We need to leave, Lisa is making us." What a man I was, blaming my wife!

At this time in my life I still didn't quite have the courage or tools to confront problems in the correct manner. I either ignored them and walked around quietly angry, sometimes for days, or I would blow up and cause a big scene. In this case I took door number two: drama. We fought the entire way home!

BATTLE ROYALE

Lisa sat in the back seat and my dad in the front passenger seat. As soon as we got in the car the battle began. We argued back and forth for a couple of hours. My poor dad, who is even quieter than me, just sat and stared straight ahead the entire time. After a few hours Lisa said she was done fighting and took a nap, then she woke up an hour later and we resumed the fight.

This was a nine-hour drive home! The fighting lasted the entire trip, and then even carried on into the night after we arrived at our house. We took a short break to see the kids off to bed and get ready ourselves, but the bickering started right back up as soon as we crawled into bed.

The war reached its peak at about 2 a.m. At this point Lisa decided she was not going to continue building the business and pursuing our dreams. She was done and yelled, "I quit! I do not want to build this business. If you want to do it, you will have to do it alone."

This was hard for me to hear. All of the fears and past storylines about failure and bad marriages came crashing into my mind. I sat on the edge of the bed and let this sink in. I had massive doubts about whether or not I could do this, especially without Lisa. I felt the bottom dropping out of my life. It was a very low moment.

In the past I would have just caved in and followed her lead, pushing my dreams down and giving up. But this time was different. All the growth I had experienced, and the newly-forming habit of listening to the voice of courage instead of the enemy voices, made me a different person in crisis. It took this challenge for me to realize how much I had changed, but when the time came, I responded very differently.

> **All the growth I had experienced, and the newly-forming habit of listening to the voice of courage instead of the enemy voices, made me a different person in crisis.**

Something inside me screamed not to give up, and for the first time I fully stood up for what I knew was right. I felt something I'd never really felt before. At that moment, sitting on the edge of the bed feeling very vulnerable, I still resolved that if I had to do this alone, I would. I looked up from the floor and my head cleared. "I'll do this alone if need be."

Something shifted. The voice of courage told me I could do this. *It will be much better if Lisa and I work on it together, of course, but I can do it if I have to. I will not quit. This is what Lisa and my family need. This is the right thing for us. We can do this. And our marriage is great. We'll pull together. I'm up to this. I'm doing it.*

The old storylines had been transformed by the growing dominance of the voice of courage in my mind, at least enough to give me the strength to change past habits. The long hours, days, and months of replacing the old voices of fear with the voice of courage had rescripted old storylines. When the crisis came, the voice of courage was no longer buried or hidden. It stood up front and center.

THE POWER OF CLEAR VISION

I looked at my wife, who by this point had been crying for several hours. I realized for the first time that this pain was being caused not by her, but by me. I was not leading my household and confronting the problems that were right in front of me. It was time I took the lead. It was time to do the right thing, and do it without making Lisa lead out again.

I looked at Lisa and said; "Okay, I will do it by myself if I have to. I believe this is the right thing for our family and if I have to I will do it alone. But I know I can be so much more with you by my side." Lisa looked up at me with tears running down her face, exhausted from crying and fighting. She seemed surprised.

"Why do you want this so badly?" she asked. "Why are we doing this?"

I put my arm around her. I looked up at the ceiling and asked myself the same question. The enemy voices were long gone. If they even tried to give voice, I shut them down immediately—over and over. The voice of courage was all I could hear.

I began to describe what our future would look like if we could push through and succeed. I said: "I can see a day, a Wednesday afternoon. It's warm and sunny, and I am headed home from a lunch meeting with some of my best friends and business partners. As I pull into our long driveway with my new Mercedes E500, I come over the hill and see our beautiful house and property.

"I walk into the house looking for you and the kids. As I approach the window I see all of you out at the horse barn getting the horses ready for a ride. We head out that afternoon and ride the trails and have a picnic as a family. This is only possible because we built a business and now are debt free, own our dream property, and have all the time in the world to spend together as a family."

I was surprised to hear these words aloud, even though such images had recently become normal for me. As the voice of courage became dominant in my mind, I found that I dreamed a lot—both during the day and while I was sleeping. But these dreams were different than the desperate longings I used to experience.

While the old dreams had usually made me feel bad, because I always experienced them along with a sense of desperation and loss, knowing they were just dreams and that they weren't likely to really happen, the new dreams were always closely connected with a sense of action. I knew that what I was doing with my days would bring these dreams—thus they were real. They made me feel happy. Actually, excited and committed is a better way to describe them.

I paused for a moment before I continued, and looked over at Lisa. She was just starring at me. She was still sobbing, but she looked entirely different than she had three minutes ago. The angry, sad sob had been replaced by tears of joy. The smile on her crying face was amazing. Now she had tears and sobs of hope and excitement!

The voice of courage had changed her from stressed and overloaded to enthusiastic. But it went even deeper now. She stared at me with such belief in me. It took my breath away. The voices of courage where joining together to help me.

As I had learned to replace all enemy voices with the voice of courage, I had begun believing in myself. But it was shocking to also, for the first time I think, see my wife looking into my eyes and entirely believing in me as well.

Then, with the same look of excitement for the future and belief in me, she said, "Okay! Let's do this then!"

For the first time in our marriage, I had the courage to confront an issue head on and lead. I could tell at that moment that Lisa, for maybe the first time, wanted to follow me. I was worthy to be followed. I was worthy to lead.

The voices in my mind came fast and furious at this point. "I need to apply what the third speaker at the seminar said... And I need to focus on that habit the Friday speaker talked about... Oh, and..." As soon as I had confronted the big challenge, the opportunity and temptation to quit, and let the voice of courage kick away the roadblocks and remain focused on the goal, and as soon as it was clear that Lisa was with me all the way, my mind just jumped right into the actions we would need to take to make our dream a reality.

That's how the voice of courage works.

It all happened so quickly, as soon as the voice of courage was fully in charge. My mind immediately engaged the roadblocks and the solutions, and went to work on what I needed to do. It's amazing what the voice of courage can do, if we reject the enemy voices long enough and fully enough to put the voice of courage entirely in charge.

PRINCIPLE 16

GO AGAINST THE CROWD

DREAMING AND THINKING WITH THE VOICE OF COURAGE LINKS WHAT YOU DREAM ABOUT WITH YOUR CURRENT ACTIONS—YOU KNOW THAT THE THINGS YOU ARE DOING NOW WILL BRING REAL RESULTS, AND THE DREAMS ARE TIED TO YOUR WORK AND ACTIONS. THIS VOICE MUST BECOME STRONGER THAN THE VOICE OF THE CROWD.

(Pay attention to how your true dreams feel, and only think and daydream in the voice of courage. Enemy voices dream in a wishy-washy way that leave you hoping you win some lottery or surprise inheritance and all your dreams suddenly come true, but deep down you feel a sense of loss because you know it will almost certainly never happen.

Also, courage dreaming is closely connected with your actions—you know you are on the right path, doing the right things, and that if you continue on this path your dreams will come. Treat the desperate dreams like what they are, enemy voices, and don't entertain them. Focus on the dreams and actions that come from the voice of courage.)

THE SOUND OF LEADERSHIP

Here's another amazing thing about the voice of courage: it is also the voice of leadership. Moreover, it always connects our dreams with action. It doesn't just dream, it focuses on the actual things we need to do to make the dreams a reality. If you are dreaming in the right voice, the voice of courage, your daydreams will include actions, things you need to do (or stop doing) to really accomplish your goals. I learned to develop the right kind of self-talk by using an affirmation statement. I wrote this statement on a note card and taped it onto the dashboard of my car. I read it aloud every time I got in or out of the car.

PRINCIPLE 17

PLAN

ALWAYS WRITE DOWN THE ACTIONS YOUR VOICE OF COURAGE GIVES YOU. REVIEW THEM DAILY, AND ACT ON THEM.

(Have a special place for this—a notebook, your phone, a 3x5 card you carry in your pocket, etc.—and keep your list of actions near. Read it every day, or better still, every morning and night, and even more often. This is your daily constitution, your life map, your blueprint of success. Keep it with you. Read it consistently. And apply it.)

I learned from all this that the right kind of confrontation, is essential to success. A leader has to make tough decisions and have the courage to confront things head on. Such situations happen over and over again in life, family, and business. Many times in my business career I had to draw on the courage to confront, and every time I did, people followed.

At one point our business was going through a transition. There was a lot of confusion. We gathered the team late one night and a business leader from another state came in to let the group know what to do. I was a new leader, rising up in the ranks, but still low enough that I was attending the meeting—not leading it.

After a few local leaders spoke, trying to assure the group that good answers would come, the visiting speaker rose to share his perspective. As he spoke, I quickly realized that he was leading the team, my team, astray. I could not just sit by and watch this happen.

> Having the character to stand for what is right is what makes for the best leader.

Following the voice of courage was new to me, and the old habits of shyness and fear of taking a stand—especially in public—tempted me to remain seated.

But the voice of courage built up inside of me, so I stood up and spoke. As I already mentioned, this was not like me at the time. But just like with Lisa on the night after our long trip and nine-hour argument, the voice of courage won. I told the visiting speaker, in front of the whole group: "We have this under control. You need to go back home and lead your team, we will take care of this team." I then shared my vision of where I thought this team was going.

The large majority of our team accepted this vision and our businesses greatly succeeded because we made the right choices and followed the voice of courage. It was far from easy, but it worked.

This kind of confrontation is never comfortable but sometimes it is the right thing to do. If you are truly immersed in learning and improving yourself, these moments become moments of truth. Having the character to stand for what is right is what makes for the best leader. The key is to help yourself and others engage the voice of courage by showing them what is possible.

PRINCIPLE 18

ACCEPT RESPONSIBILITY

WHEN YOU NEED TO CONFRONT SOMETHING OR SOMEONE, REMEMBER THAT THE GOAL ISN'T TO PROVE THAT YOU ARE RIGHT AND THEY ARE WRONG; THE TOP GOAL IS GET EVERYONE ON THE SAME PAGE—SEEING THE BEST VISION OF WHAT IS POSSIBLE, WHAT OUR WORK WILL BRING, AND WHY THE EFFORT IS ALL WORTH IT.

(Take responsibility for making things better. Confrontation isn't ultimately about winning; at its best it is about getting everyone to feel the voice of courage and realize what's possible! This is a game-changer.)

STAY REAL

Replacing all self-defeating voices with the voice of courage doesn't make everything easy. Success is hard. Period. In fact, this is where many people stumble. For example, several years ago a number of books about the power of our minds became best-sellers. They taught that the key to success in life, finances, relationships, etc. is to get your mind positive and keep it there. A lot of people bought these books, read them, and tried to follow their advice.

But then hard things happened to them on the way toward success. Hard things happen in this life to everyone, whether you're chasing your dream or stuck in a rut, or anywhere in between. That's just part of life. But many people who thought they'd discovered the secrets of success became discour-

> **Hard things happen in this life to everyone, whether you're chasing your dream or stuck in a rut, or anywhere in between. That's just part of life.**

aged. They didn't actually fight the very difficult battle to make the voice of courage the truly dominant voice in their life. They just tried to be positive, and when hard things came they listened to the numerous self-defeating voices that bombard all of us.

Let's get this straight. Self-defeating voices constantly attack all of us, all of the time. Successful people learn to always replace these voices with the voice of courage. Always. They make this a habit. But this doesn't end the problems, roadblocks, difficulties and challenges of life. Not at all. There is no royal road to success, no easy way to truly become who you were born to be. It takes work. As bestselling author Chris Brady said: "It will probably take all you have to become everything you were meant to be." We simply must engage the battle to make the voice of courage our dominant voice in life.

Stick with the habit of listening only to the voice of courage, and it will greatly help you deal with life's problems and tragedies. But it won't put an end to them. They'll keep coming. That's life.

Notice that successful people live and succeed in real life, just like everyone else. They just learn to deal with life using the voice of courage, not the self-defeating voices that hold us back and tear us down. Making the voice of courage your dominant voice isn't some secret road to easy street, it's a ton of hard work. And you have to keep at it for life.

Moreover, as mentioned above, the voice of courage doesn't give you "dreams for the sake of dreaming." It really wants you to achieve your dreams. Thus it gives you actions right along with any dreams. And it takes courage to act on these things, and to keep acting on them when life gets hard.

THE STRUGGLE

When you build the habit of always replacing any enemy voices with the voice of courage, and you make the voice of courage your dominant voice—day in and day out—it gives you true dreams and the actions you need to take to make them real. This is all wonderful, and powerful. Most people don't make it this far. But this isn't enough.

Why? Because at this point you'll be doing something most people don't do: you'll be daydreaming and thinking in the voice of courage. This means you are taking some amazing actions because you feel the power of your dream.

But most people around you are doing something different. As a leader, you'll frequently find yourself asking them to take the same amazing actions in their lives as you are, but you must remember that they are trying to do so without feeling the power of the dream. Specifically: They are being asked to work and sacrifice to take amazing actions, but most of them are doing it while living with the dominant voices of fear, self-doubt, and the inner critic.

So, what to do? This is where leadership comes in. You (living in the dominant voice of courage) need to help those you lead do the same. First, you can teach them the principles of listening only to the right voice, like the principles outlined in this book—teach them how to effectively replace the voices of fear and self-criticism with the voice of courage, and how to make the voice of courage the dominant voice in their lives.

Second, and this is crucial, help them envision the real goal. They need to see what their dream feels like, tastes like, smells like. Paint the picture for them in living color.

And the only way to do this is to tell them *your* dream—one that also includes them—your dream from the voice of courage. Tell it to them in a way they can't help but grasp it. When you show them your dream by sharing it the right way, they'll naturally hear the voice of courage in your words and turn to their own voice of courage for the dream it has to share with them.

> **And the only way to do this is to tell them your dream—one that also includes them—your dream from the voice of courage.**

Consider the way I shared my dream with Lisa:

"I can see a day, a Wednesday afternoon. It's a warm sunny day, and I am headed home from a lunch meeting with some of my best friends and business partners. As I pull into our long driveway with my new Mercedes E500, I come over the hill and see our beautiful house and property.

"I walk into the house looking for you and the kids. As I approach the window I see all of you out at the horse barn getting the horses ready for a ride. We head out that afternoon and ride the trails and have a picnic as a family. This is only possible because we built a business and now are debt free, own our dream property, and have all the time in the world to spend together as a family."

These words changed things for Lisa and I. The voice of courage, once I made it the dominant voice in my life, put this vision into my heart and mind. With these words and vision there, it was impossible for me to quit—even when things got extremely hard.

I knew, from the voice of courage and from mentors who had already achieved success, that the things we were doing to build our business would eventually bring this dream, and to quit the business meant to give up on this dream. So I simply could not quit.

I was fiercely committed to doing the hard work and overcoming the hard challenges, because I wanted this dream with all my heart.

Never!

I was fiercely committed to doing the hard work and overcoming the hard challenges, because I wanted this dream with all my heart. When I learned to share these words with others, over time, it helped them naturally connect with their own individual dreams, and this gave them the courage to pursue them.

Leadership means helping people do the actions of success and learn to combine them with the dream of success, and also with a long-term habit of listening only to the dominant voice of courage. Not everyone will choose this path, but leadership is about helping as many people as possible do so.

We sometimes need to walk others through their thinking, helping them reframe how they see the struggle. When a leader listening to the voice of courage reframes the story, it helps the people you lead understand how the voice of courage speaks. Many people have never heard the voice of courage, or haven't allowed it to lead. You can tell them their story through your eyes by using the voice of courage.

RECAP

- When a problem, argument, difficulty or other challenge comes, especially if you are tempted to quit, you are likely on the verge of a breakthrough. If you step up and stay on the path, refusing to give up, you'll find out what the breakthrough is and how much it can help you.

- The right kinds of dreams don't get you down, or cause you to feel loss because you know they're "only a dream." Instead, the right kinds of dreams are closely connected with the actions you take and the work you are doing to make the dreams into reality.

- When you listen to the voice of courage enough that it becomes the voice of your dream, and you keep doing the work that comes with the dream, you are on the right path.

- Write down the actions your voices of courage (and good mentors) give you. Keep them with you, and read them often—at least every morning and night. These are your blueprint or map for success. Again: Keep them close and read them often.

- Take courage and confront things that need to be confronted. Face them head on.

- Remember that the purpose of most confrontation isn't to prove that you are right, but to get everyone to see the best option and buy in to what is best. Always confront accordingly.

- Self-defeating voices never stop bombarding us. Successful people simply replace all such voices with the voice of courage. They do this immediately and consistently. They make this a habit. It is a choice.

- Life has many difficulties and challenges, for everyone. Successful people respond to these challenges in the voice of courage.

- Don't think that by listening to the voice of courage you can make everything in your life suddenly easy. Struggle is part of life. Courage helps us deal with struggle, not eliminate all problems. There is no secret, easy road to success. Successful people fully engage the voice of courage and use it to face and overcome their struggles.

- Knowing your dream is powerful. Share it with others who are trying to build their dreams and want your help, and share it in a way they'll understand by painting a picture of what your dream looks and feels like. This helps them picture their own dreams.

CHAPTER 6

THE COURAGE OF CHARACTER

"Never give in..."
—Winston Churchill

hen we know we are on the right path, giving up isn't an option. We must persevere. The path of courage and success makes even more sense when we deeply understand the concept of true *character*. I was taught early on that there is a difference between integrity and character. Integrity is about knowing what's right, while character is doing what's right.

For example: Let's say my daughter comes home one day and says that a group of girls were gossiping about another girl behind her back. My daughter says that when this occurred she was upset and knew it was wrong and didn't participate in it herself. She had integrity. However, my question would be: "Did you do anything to stop it?" If so, that would be character. If not, the integrity fell short of character.

Having character requires courage. It takes guts to not only know what is wrong, and right, but to stand up and take action—to *do* what is right, especially when it is very hard, unpopular, dangerous, or risky in some way.

PRINCIPLE 19

BELIEVE

THE VOICE OF CHARACTER IS THE VOICE OF COURAGE. BELIEVING IN CHARACTER, AND ACTING ALWAYS ON THIS BELIEF, IS KEY TO ANY REAL SUCCESS.

(Building your character means aligning your life, choices, and actions always with the voice of courage— and believing that this will bring you the best results.)

When you see character in action it makes you want to stand and fight with the person leading out. I have been blessed with a wife, mentors, and colleagues who live this way. Their strength of character gives me strength. I remember being in a boardroom with a bunch of lawyers and my business partners. We were in the process of starting a new company and establishing the ground-work for this new venture.

At one point in the meeting one of the attorneys was working on a clause, one that was questionable in our eyes but would be legal and very profitable for us. Before the attorney could finish speaking my partners and I started feeling uneasy. We knew our purpose in starting this business was to help people, not just make money. We interrupted the attorney and changed direction. The great thing about this: it was unanimous.

I admire this level of character. When people are willing to sacrifice personal gain for what is right, every time, real character and real leadership are at play. In fact, character is inspiring. It was unanimous leadership. Unanimous character. The voice of courage was in charge.

As we discussed the topic further, everyone agreed on ways do things right, and pushed back when anything less was mentioned by the attorneys or experts. It is moments like this that make me so proud to be in business with these people. I have seen them make very tough decisions, and every time their character shines through.

> **It seems like most of the problems I ran into in life occurred because I lacked the courage to confront the real issue head on.**

They became this way by letting the voice of courage dominate their lives. And this is not an easy task—it takes great work and continual effort. The voice of courage, when it becomes the long-term dominant voice in our lives, is the voice of impeccable character.

The question we each need to ask of ourselves is: Am I that kind of leader? When you have a tough situation, do you stand up and confront it, fighting for what is right, or do you justify not saying anything, or going along with a lesser way? In the long term, you won't be a real leader and you won't have anyone following you if you don't learn to confront the issues in the right way. Meaning: with the voice of courage, the voice of character.

It seems like most of the problems I ran into in life occurred because I lacked the courage to confront the real issue head on. However, there has always been a part inside of me that wanted to do right. It is essential to let the voice of courage speak, and to make it the dominant voice in our lives.

This is the only way to become the kind of leaders we truly want to be. Again, making the voice of courage the dominant voice in life isn't one path to leadership and real success—it is the *only* path.

THE COURAGE TO CHANGE

Like the courage of character, the courage to change is also an essential part of leadership and success. Those who don't change can't achieve real success in life.

> **Like the courage of character, the courage to change is also an essential part of leadership and success.**

Change is a funny thing, actually. Everyone wants things to change, as long as someone else does the changing. To put this in personal terms, Joe wants to change as long as his wife will do things differently and Joe gets to enjoy the benefits. But if Joe has to change his personal habits and long-held opinions, the idea of changing is often a lot less palatable to him.

This is illustrated in a very public way right now as I'm working on this book. Our government is in massive debt and pretty much everyone agrees that we need need to make changes and cut back on spending. However, every time some official tries to make cuts there is an uprising around the nation.

If the government wants to cut program A, one party throws a tantrum. If the government tries to cut program B, the other party has a fit. Every special interest lobby on K Street thinks it knows exactly what things we should cut, and which we shouldn't cut—but these same special interests nearly all disagree about the specifics.

Most neighborhoods have the same problem. Everyone knows there needs to be cuts, they just want the cuts to hurt someone else. Elderly groups don't want to cut anything that reduces their benefits, and organizations representing families with children like the programs that help their kids. "Cut those other programs," we all tend to say. "They won't impact me all." This has become a national mantra.

This gets repeated over and over. "Don't cut anything that reduces my benefits. But cut a lot. Cut deeply. And fast. Just cut other peoples' programs, of course."

It's a mess, because nobody wants to change in ways that inconvenience them personally. At the same time, they want to cut things—a lot! As a nation, we want to have our cake and eat it too. A lot of other nations are in the same boat as well.

More to the point, a lot of people experience this same problem on a personal level. We know we need to change, but we want to avoid any pain or inconvenience. It's ironic, really. We know we should change, but we hope we can do so without bother, difficulty, or struggle.

Yet change is meant to be a struggle. If we don't struggle, we aren't actually changing.

THE VOICE OF CHANGE

Of course, the real battle behind all this is the internal struggle of competing fear-based voices. We are afraid of change because we fear pain and bad outcomes. None of this is built on the voice of courage.

The right voice tells a very different story. It focuses on what we really want. Something better than what we have now. Our true dream. It begins with the end in mind, to quote Stephen Covey.

This is a powerful beginning point. If nations would begin with the dream in mind, it would make a huge difference. Imagine your nation free of government debt, much lower taxes, much less waste, programs that are truly effective and accomplish just what they are meant to, a flourishing economy with much more prosperity and opportunity, more plentiful jobs, higher pay, etc.

Whatever the real dream, or goal, that's the place to start. If we did this as a nation, and came together on what we really want, it would be much easier for all the various groups to support making the needed sacrifices to get there. This is the difference between real

> **Change is meant to be a struggle. If we don't struggle, we aren't actually changing.**

leadership and mere management. Until the people buy in to a shared dream, nobody will want to change anything that impacts them directly—they'll just want others to change.

Individual change is very similar: We must get a clear vision of what dream we are seeking. As long as our dreams are a battling struggle between the voices of fear, self-criticism, underlying false storylines, and other self-defeating voices, even with the occasional thought from the voice of courage thrown in, we'll stay in flux.

We'll battle inside, and tend to live in a rut on the outside. Finances and relationships will struggle, not toward greatness, but just in a constant inner battle of fear-based stirring and avoiding— trying at best to make ends meet, not even seeking to actually build lasting prosperity or wealth.

The contrast is stark. When we focus on the voice of courage, change is exciting. We have a dream, and the voice of courage quickly and effectively sets out actions that will move us toward the dream. Then we take action. Not fearfully, but enthusiastically— because the actions of change are so closely connected to our goals and dreams.

Of course, it gets hard, and we run into a roadblock. The voice of courage admits the setback, then immediately looks for ways to turn it into an opportunity. More enthusiasm, more action, more hard work. But always forward with momentum, moving toward the dream.

A problem arises, or an illness, an accident, a mistake, an attack, a lost friend or supporter, etc. Whatever comes, the voice of courage takes stock, sees the reality, and recommends the path that will most effectively move us to the dream. If the path is a "road not taken," or "less traveled," the rocky climb up the steepest peak, so be it. The voice of courage grins and then steps forward. It may frown as well as smile, or cry, or even sob, but always forward. It takes real action toward the goal.

The twists and turns of life, when the voice of courage is in charge, in no way resemble the circular, spinning, troubled ruts of life that occur when the self-defeating voices are at the helm. The latter takes us round and round, sometimes holding serve or hitting par, other times spiraling downward, but seldom creating progress or building anything that lasts.

Living paycheck to paycheck, economists call it. Mathematicians refer to it as a repeating decimal. Some artists paint over and over on an already used canvass, because none of the old paintings are worth keeping. In auto mechanics we know that too many things are just planned obsolescence.

The voice of courage does it differently. Where the purpose of self-defeating voices is simply to keep us from achieving our greatness, the voice of courage has other plans. It wants us to live our dream. To achieve our best life. To build, to serve, to change the world for good.

THE REAL COST

To accomplish these ends, the voice of courage needs us to change. We need to become masters of change, willing to change, skilled at change—ready to take action when change is needed. The voice of courage isn't identical to the voice of change, because it isn't interested in change just for the sake of change. It only wants the right changes, the ones that move us toward the dream.

PRINCIPLE 20

EMBRACE HARD

THE VOICE OF COURAGE TELLS US TO CHANGE WHENEVER CHANGE IS NEEDED TO MOVE US TOWARD OUR DREAM—TO CONSISTENTLY PUT ASIDE THE WRONG VOICES AND DO DIFFICULT THINGS.

(This kind of change can be hard, but it is exactly what we want—it is the kind of change that brings real results.)

When people say that change is hard, they are right. Or they are wrong, depending on what they mean. On the one hand, change is hard because struggle can be hard and because life is sometimes hard. Thus as life unfolds, hard things come to us. In this way, change is hard.

But the kind of change that works with the voice of courage is actually quite exciting and fulfilling. Yes, it comes with its share of hard, because it is part of life. But we would experience hard things even if we never listened to the voice of courage. When we do listen, however, the hard things that occur are frequently part of building what we really want. This is the kind of hard that is worth it.

For example, it is no harder to *swing* the bat than to sit with it on your shoulder, just like it is really no harder to run around the bases after hitting a home run than it is to walk back to the dugout after striking out without even swinging. But one is so much better than the other.

The truth is that a person who doesn't understand baseball, or physiology, might believe that the easiest, less difficult route to the dugout is straight from home plate to the bench, rather than running all the way around the bases and then to the dugout. But this misses the entire point of the game. Yes, it takes about four times as many steps to go around the bases, and running expends much more energy than walking slowly to the bench after a strikeout, but who wouldn't rather hit the home run?

Likewise, living our dreams does demand some extra work and effort. But in the long run, isn't the extra time with family, the extra income, the opportunities for leadership, the successful achievement of your goals, or whatever other benefits your dream brings you, worth it?

So many people settle for what seems easier in the short term instead of going after what is actually much better, more fun, and a more rewarding life in the long term. Most people take the easy but lesser path. Thus the world is often made up of the "10 percent" versus the "90 percent", or the 1 person in line versus the 300, as we discussed in earlier chapters.

> **So many people settle for what seems easier in the short term instead of going after what is actually much better, more fun, and a more rewarding life in the long term.**

Only a few people go after their dream and live it, because only a few people make the voice of courage their dominant voice, get mentors who do the same, and then live by the voice of courage—and the actions it gives them—day in and day out.

LABELS

Another hard change that the voice of courage sometimes asks of us is to overcome labels. This can be difficult. For example, for years I labeled myself as "Only a Mechanic." I didn't say, "I'm a mechanic," very often, but rather "I'm only a mechanic." The word "only" was a label I wore on my sleeve like a scarlet letter.

It was my shame and my excuse, all at the same time. It allowed me to bow my head, avoid saying more or engaging with people, and spend more time with my TV.

The truth is that some mechanics are living their life purpose and living their dreams. The world needs great mechanics. Some build their own business, others run their own shop, and love to focus on the daily work and provide a vital service to others. Some mechanics make a living working on cars but fulfill their life missions serving young people as a soccer coach or youth pastor. Others serve in other ways, really making a positive difference in the world.

My problem had nothing to do with being a mechanic. It had everything to do with becoming a mechanic when I had other dreams, and with settling for this job just because my step dad owned a shop and made it easy. My issue wasn't being a mechanic, but being "only a mechanic," which is how I labeled myself.

As a matter of fact, working for my step dad taught me many lessons that were a huge blessing later on when I decided to build my own business. He taught me how to run a business with character and focus on serving and communicating with the customers. I watched him time and again put the customers' interests over his own.

Still, even though I learned some wonderful things, being a mechanic wasn't the path I really wanted to pursue in life. I kept looking for something different.

But the inner critic wasn't easy to overcome. As I was struggling to replace all self-defeating voices with the voice of courage, and also rescript false storylines with the voice of courage, I additionally had to learn that the voice of negative labels was an enemy as well. Every time I thought of myself as "only a mechanic," or "just a mechanic," or "what do you expect from me?—after all, I'm a mechanic, nothing more," I had to replace this thought with the voice of courage.

> **As you fight this battle to make and keep the voice of courage your dominant voice, remember that change happens over time, not overnight.**

I told you already that we learned to be all in, 100 percent committed to the voice of courage, and this included overcoming certain labels I had given myself or accepted from others. If you have any labels that hold you back in any way, it is important to realize that they are enemy voices. Replace them with the voice of courage.

As you fight this battle to make and keep the voice of courage your dominant voice, remember that change happens over time, not overnight. There is a double meaning to this, in fact. First, real changes occur over time, meaning that you have to keep replacing all self-defeating voices with the voice of courage throughout your life. This battle never ends. Always fight it. As you keep winning it, you stay on the path of success. It does get easier as you create the right habits of consulting the voice of courage, because now that voice becomes the first to speak.

Also, we don't have to expect perfection as we go, just progress.

Second, a little extra overtime work on this is very helpful, meaning that it's valuable to tell yourself: "I'm going to pay close attention to my thoughts and feelings, and any time I feel negative, I'm going to immediately turn to the voice of courage and listen to what it tells me." This is good overtime effort—every day. It deserves overtime pay, which is what you get (in increased effectiveness) when you make this a true habit.

EYES OPEN!

In short, as we fight the battle of success, a number of things can sneak up on us and surprise us. It's as if the self-defeating voices in our minds are constantly looking for ways to trick us into listening to them again.

If we face all the varieties of enemy voices and tricks head on and replace them with the voice of courage, they try to run around our efforts and sneak up on us using arguments with loved ones, new difficulties or hardships in life, old labels we once bought into, the natural tendency to avoid changing, character tests where we are tempted to put profit or self-interest before what we know to be right, and so on.

We must remain vigilant. We must keep the voice of courage forefront in our mind, whatever happens and whatever comes.

This is the voice of success, the voice of power, and the voice of our best life.

No matter what happens in life, the voice of courage is the right state of mind. It is our best self. It may seem like a small thing to always keep the voice of courage dominant, but it isn't. It is the key thing. It makes all the difference.

Those who do this have courage. Those who keep doing it develop the character and courage to overcome.

RECAP

- Know when you are on the right path, and when you are, always persevere. This is a key part of having real character.

- Character is the long-term voice of courage. Develop your character by always replacing enemy voices with the voice of courage.

- The voice of courage teaches us to change as needed to achieve our goals and live our dream. This kind of change is very different than the change (or not changing) recommended by the voices of self-doubt, the inner-critic, etc. The right kind of change makes us better, and it is ultimately more fun and brings more success and happiness than not changing.

- Treat any labels that hold you back like the enemy voices they are. Replace them with the voice of courage.

- Whatever happens in life, we must respond to it from the voice of courage. This is a crucial facet of success.

- The voices of self-doubt, fear, and the inner critic, among others, seek ways to convince, trick, and even deceive us into giving them more power than the voice of courage. Successful people are vigilant and effectively resist such efforts and schemes.

CONCLUSION

THE COURAGE TO ENCOURAGE

"Fear is the mind killer..."
—Frank Herbert

The spotlights made it almost impossible to see the whole crowd. The music was playing loudly, "Voice of Truth" by Casting Crowns. Lisa and I had just walked to the podium. A huge arena of people were on their feet, cheering. Even without the spotlights, I couldn't have picked out all the faces—certainly not clear up on the third deck, standing high above the floor in the large throng of humanity. I could hardly make out individual faces at the back part of the chairs on the main floor—they seemed like a football field away.

I was ready to speak, but the cheering continued. The clapping was a potent uproar of enthusiasm. I wondered how many decibels the arena could handle.

I tried to get the crowd's attention, but the microphone wasn't strong enough to overpower the waves of cheering. I leaned away from the microphone and the audience renewed its welcoming applause. It got even louder.

I grinned. Lisa was smiling. I reached over and held her hand, and kissed her cheek. Although I wanted to begin, the lump in my throat made it hard to speak. I was on the verge of tears as the last few years flashed in my mind. All of the pain, all of the critics, the challenges, the ups and downs—and always the great battle between the voices of fear and self-doubt versus my voice of courage. I took a deep breath and looked at the huge audience. "How can I possibly reach them?" I wondered. "I really want to help them." Then I grinned and told myself: "You win."

The voice of courage filled me with so much excitement. "I can help these people so much." I couldn't wait to start sharing my message. The voice in my mind pushed past the din of the crowd and focused on the topic I was speaking about: The mechanics of leadership and success...

A catch in my throat stopped me. I doubt anyone else noticed how deeply I felt this. Putting the words "mechanic" and "success" in the same sentence brought up a lot of emotions inside me. I looked around the room again. The people were still cheering.

"I thought I'd spend my life in a small shop working quietly with cars," the words came randomly to my mind. I grinned again. That was the path I had been on for so many years, the path I once thought was my only option, the road I once believed would last my entire life. I shook my head. "That wasn't my true path at all." I smiled. "This is my path."

The mechanics of success and leadership are simple. Get them right, and everything else will fall into place. But try to succeed without them, and everything will fall apart.

Success. I lingered over the word. Why does something so simple require so much hard work to understand and master? Thomas Paine got it right: Heaven knows how to put a proper price on things, and success demands everything we have to give. But it makes us so much better in the process. It requires our all, and gives us so much more than we put in.

I looked at the cheering crowd. How to get everyone in this room to understand this, and to take the right action to live their dreams? I took a deep breath. I smiled again. I looked at Lisa once more, then at the crowd. I began to speak…

> **The mechanics of success and leadership are simple. Get them right, and everything else will fall into place. But try to succeed without them, and everything will fall apart.**

FORKS IN THE ROAD

It really is so simple, after all is said and done. We have to understand and live twenty principles. This brings the mindset for success. It's not easy—not even close. It is incredibly hard. But so is sitting back and not succeeding. So is leaving the bat on your shoulder and wondering the rest of your life, "What if I would have taken a *swing*?"

As I already said, life is sometimes hard, for everyone. The path to success isn't more difficult than the path to failure. Yes, the run around the bases is different than the long walk back to the dugout after striking out. But it isn't more difficult.

In fact, it's a lot better. For that matter, so is the walk back to the dugout after swinging like mighty Casey and missing. Somehow you just walk with your head held higher than you would if you

had watched the pitches float past and didn't even try to *swing*. I've
done both, and one is much more enjoyable.

Swing enough, and the homeruns will come. And running
around the bases is…well, it's a whole lot easier in the long run
than standing with the bat on your shoulder.

Twenty principles. Each is powerful all on its own. Together they
are a lifestyle. In my life they were a revolution. An epic journey. A
mutiny, even. A full-blown rebellion against my former life and my
early personal trajectory toward a lifetime of mediocrity.

I could have so easily stayed in the mechanic shop.

I wonder, as I'm driving home today, what my life would be like
if I had never chosen the voice of courage. What if I were still on
that old path, after all these years? What would my life be?

I try to answer this question in my mind…

Must See TV would now be TGIT (Thank God it's
Thursday), the motto of another network. I guess I'd have a
new set of favorite TV programs to serve as the weekly highlight of my life. I don't even know what the popular shows
are anymore.

Then horror strikes: Who would I be without all the
friends I've made, the great people I call brother, the relationships Lisa and I have built with so many close mentors and
colleagues? And how would my false storyline of "Marriage
is Bad" have hurt my family by now? I shudder to think of it.

My mom once told Lisa, while driving back from a
business meeting: "I was certain you and Dan would get a
divorce, never make it. Now look at you." Would we have

gotten divorced if I never learned to follow the voice of courage?

Honestly, I can hardly even stomach the thought. The other things, like cars and houses and travel (or not) give me a tiny bit of pause, but it's how my marriage and family would be different that really shakes me. I honestly believe our last 3 children would have not even been brought into this world because of our struggles.

Would my false scripting of being quiet, fearful, and shy dominate my life in this alternate reality? The answer is immediate. Of course it would. I don't know how it would have played out, exactly, but it wouldn't have been good.

What about a life with much less free time to spend with Lisa and the girls? I shake my head. That would be horrible. What an irretrievable loss.

We all come to forks in the road of life, and we make choices. I tremble a bit whenever I wonder what would have happened if I'd stayed on that earlier path.

I smile, back in the present. I feel so blessed. Even after all the hard work. The tears. The sobs. The struggles. The phone calls, the meetings, the driving. The times we wanted to quit.

Then I remember. The worst thing of all would be to feel the way I usually felt back then. To be tossed about by the voices of fear, the inner critic, and false labels and storylines in my gut. To never truly know the voice of courage, the real me. To seldom dream, except to wish the lottery or something like it would come and rescue me—knowing all along that it wouldn't.

That's enough. I replace this foray into an alternative universe with the voice of courage. It is focused and knows what's important.

What needs to be done today? How can I improve the way I... What does Lisa need from me the most this week? Who in my business needs my help today...and what is the best way to help them? Is it time to...

I take mental notes and plan for tomorrow. Then I begin reminiscing again: I'm living my dream. I love my life. This is who I was born to be, and what I was born to do. Has it been hard? Yes. At times it was devastatingly hard. And we learned so much.

Will hard things come again? Of course. And we'll face them like we always do, together, with the voice of courage leading the way.

I smile again. I steer my Mercedes E500 into the driveway and head for the horse barn. We live in the exact house I visited many years ago and that inspired the dream I shared with Lisa on the night I decided the voice of courage would always be my dominant voice. The exact house!

I had kept my eye on this place, even when affording it was nothing but a pipe dream. The house and property were sold to different owners twice over the years as we built our business, and when we could finally afford it, the estate miraculously came back on the market.

"Be careful what you aim for," I tell myself. "If you live in the voice of courage, it can come true."

I park the car and get out, taking in the beautiful trees and fields, and the eight-car repair shop I keep around just for fun. I can hear my family in the barn. We're going on a ride today with the whole family. I think Lisa and the girls packed a picnic.

PAY IT FORWARD

I want more people to live the dream inside their heart. But I know this will never happen unless they learn and apply the twenty principles outlined above. There are many different dreams—at least one for each and every person. Some are financial or family-ori-

> **Whatever your dream, living it means finding and fully embracing the voice of courage.**

ented, others have to do with art or music, science or technology, service or improving the world, and so on.

A friend of mine loves golf, another loves the financial freedom to fly to Spain with his son to watch their favorite soccer player in person, and another wants to spread the principles of freedom and good government worldwide. Still another dreams of helping millions of families get entirely out of debt, and another yearns to help people connect more deeply with their faith.

Whatever your dream, living it means finding and fully embracing the voice of courage. It means immersing yourself for life in the twenty principles above. It means doing more than learning about them—it requires living them.

My dream now is to help other people live their dream. I want them to know how to do this, how to build something that lasts and supports their true goals, and how to transform themselves into effective and inspiring leaders who live all twenty principles each day. I want them to have what Lisa and I now have, a change in direction, a new path that really works, and a dream life that is a daily reality.

I want them to have more time to spend with the people they really love, a flourishing financial outlook that allows them to do what they really want in life, and the ability to look around and serve people in ways they only dreamed about in the past. I want to encourage them, to show them how simple the path of success really is, and to assure them that the results of success are worth the struggles and hardships that come along the way.

JUST IMAGINE

Imagine a world where everyone goes after his or her dreams, and keeps at it, learning along the way, until success is earned and achieved. This is a very different world than the one we currently occupy, but it doesn't have to be. So many people in the line of 300 can switch lines, head the other direction, and chase their dreams.

Sadly, we live in a world where most people are afraid to even encourage others to make this switch. It's like most of us are sitting in the bleachers yelling to each other, as each person takes his or her turn at bat: "Don't *swing*. Keep the bat on your shoulder. Don't try to change or improve. Just settle for whatever you've got. Don't try for more."

> **Without the voice of courage, there would certainly be no entrepreneurship, and the world would be burdened with more misery, poverty, and pain. We need the voice of courage.**

Has our whole society gone mad? Why is this our natural position? Why do so many people frequently counsel their youth, friends, and everyone else against seeking for more, going after their dreams, swinging for the fence? Why don't more of us have the courage to encourage?

The answer is simple, and sobering. We are a society addicted to the voices of fear, doubt, and self-criticism. The voice of courage is so surprising to most people nowadays that when they hear it they feel an immediate sense of shock. Even outrage. The voice of courage strikes too many people today like a threat. We panic. We may even take offense.

Think of it! As a society we've moved so far in the direction of avoiding the voice of courage that any hint of it feels insulting. Dangerous. Even irresponsible.

It's like the story of the young man in an elite private prep school who, when the teacher asked the whole class what colleges they were hoping to attend, replied that he was joining the Marine Corps. After hearing the other responses, from Harvard and Brown to Magdalen College or Yale and Wharton, the idea of military service brought stares of shock. Nobody was prepared for such an answer, and nobody, including the teacher, knew what to say. The few who tried to respond simply attempted to talk him out of such an alarming and "ridiculous" plan.

Another young man in a university business course experienced a similar response. The professor asked all class members to share their career goals upon graduation. Most students spoke of jobs they wanted, or graduate studies, or even a gap year of traveling around Europe. When his turn came, this freshman told the group he intended to build an entrepreneurial sales business and become a millionaire.

The professor immediately laughed out loud. But the rest of the class didn't think it was funny. They were upset, and spent the rest of the hour taking turns trying to talk him out of his plans. They called his goals impossible, improbable, even stupid. Many seemed deeply offended that he would say such a thing at all. Not because they disliked his goal, but because they saw it as unreachable. "Get real..." was repeated a number of times.

Sadly, the voice of courage is too seldom part of our public dialogue. It even struggles to make its way into private conversations. None of this should be too surprising, I guess, given how difficult it is to get past the dominant voices of fear and self-defeat in our own personal thoughts and feelings.

THE NEED

Yet it is this very voice of courage that brings any improvement or progress to our world. This voice launched the Mayflower, went with Washington to Valley Forge, and stood with the marines on Iwo Jima. It stormed the beaches at Normandy, spoke out against slavery in the 1850s, and stood up for truth in a thousand little churches around the world during times of religious persecution. It runs through every page of the Bible.

Without this voice we would have no Magna Carta and no Declaration of Independence. Canada, America, and the Caribbean would not have been colonized, and nobody would have taken to the seas or visited the many islands or frontiers around the globe. The mountains would remain unclimbed, the rivers uncharted. We wouldn't have even tried to go to the moon.

Without the voice of courage, there would certainly be no entrepreneurship, and the world would be burdened with more misery, poverty, and pain. We need the voice of courage. It brings a spark to the eyes of fathers and mothers, and bonds families and communities more tightly together. It looks around, sees what is needed in the world, and takes action to greatly improve things.

We not only need to engage the voice of courage personally, in our own lives, we also need to have the courage to encourage. We should frequently invite others to do the same.

It is said that Dante Gabriel Rossetti, the famous 19th century poet and artist, was once approached by an elderly man. The old fellow had some sketches and drawings that he had created, and he wanted Rossetti to look at them and tell him if they were any good, or if they at least showed potential talent.

Rossetti looked them over carefully. After the first few, he knew they were worthless, showing not the least sign of artistic talent. But Rossetti was a kind man, and he told the elderly man as gently as possible that the pictures were of limited, if any, value. He was sorry, but he could not lie to the man.

> **We not only need to engage the voice of courage personally, in our own lives, we also need to have the courage to encourage.**

The visitor was disappointed, but seemed to have expected Rossetti's judgment.

He then apologized for taking up the great artist's time, but asked if he would just look at a few more drawings that had been done by a much younger art student. Rossetti looked over the second batch of sketches and immediately became enthusiastic over the talent they revealed.

"These," he said, "Oh, these are good. This young student has great talent. He should be given every help and encouragement in his career as an artist. He has a great future if he will work hard and stick to it."

Rossetti could see that the old fellow was deeply moved. "Who is this fine young artist?" he asked. "Your son?"

"No," said the old man sadly. "It is me, 40 years ago. If only I had heard your praise then! For you see, I got discouraged and gave up—too soon."

Encouragement can make such a difference for people.

When I was born, many babies were dying of SIDS, and my mom was gripped by fear and could hardly leave me alone in my crib to sleep. She went as far as using a mirror under my nose repeatedly to see if I was still breathing.

One night she prayed that the fear would be removed, but only if God had plans for me to grow, follow Him and do something significant with my life. She slept soundly that night and awoke happily to my cries the next morning. From that day on she would tell me that God had good plans for me. Someday I would be a teacher, leader and very successful.

She repeated these words to me often throughout my life. When I chose to be a mechanic, she said, "I am not sure how this will happen as a mechanic, but someday you will be a teacher, leader, and successful." In some of the darkest moments of my life those words carried me through the day. In moments when I wanted the quit, the voice of courage recalled those words and stiffened my resolve.

Never underestimate the power of your encouragement to others. Encourage them to listen to the right voice, the voice of courage.

Yes, it is true that the voice of courage points us in the direction of risk. Just like swinging my bat was risky. After all, the pitcher might have just walked me—I might have gotten on base without even needing to *swing*.

But life doesn't work that way. Even if I had been walked that day as I stood with bat on shoulder, I would have failed, because swinging is what makes life worth living. Chasing our dreams is what makes us into the kind of people who can handle those dreams when they do come. After all, most lottery winners end up broke within a few years.[13] We learn how to truly live our dreams by earning them. Our struggles don't only turn our dreams into realities, they also make us into the people we need to be in order to make the most of such dreams.

People who are given money, fame, or position, but still live in a mind dominated by the voices of fear, self-criticism, and self-attack, are just as miserable as those without such privileges. They may focus their self-defeating voices on different things, but they still hold themselves back from lives of happiness, leadership, and success.

The truth is that everyone wants and needs to learn about the voice of courage—to make it their dominant voice, and to live their best life. Most people don't do this, but it is still our true potential. And almost anyone can do it. The twenty

> **We learn how to truly live our dreams, by earning them.**

principles outlined above are that powerful, and that effective.

Sadly, however, only a few people choose to make this exciting change. Part of the problem, as mentioned, is that the voice of courage is too seldom heard in our homes, schools, and communities. We hide the voice of courage, and secretly hope it will show up if it is ever needed. When it does arise, we frequently try to tamp it back down, like a societal game of whack-a-mole, afraid it might lead someone down a risky path.

Then we are surprised to see so much weakness, mediocrity, and evil in our world. As C.S. Lewis put it in his book *The Abolition of Man*: "We laugh at honor and are shocked to find traitors in our midst. We castrate and bid the geldings be fruitful." We teach many of our young to follow the easiest path, to avoid risk, to fit in with every crowd, and then we are surprised when mediocrity is the norm.

Note that when C.S. Lewis wrote this, he was teaching us how to evaluate books—to determine whether they are good books or not. The great books, he pointed out, speak in the voice of courage. He didn't use this exact phrase, instead his wording was "men with chests," referring to books that teach young readers to have heart, courage, and valor in the face of temptation, trials, opportunities, and the difficulties of life.

We need to become encouragers, and to promote more success, leadership, and the pursuit of dreams by more frequently sharing the voice of courage. This is missing in far too many lives and nations. The ideas of courage and encourage naturally go together.

Have the courage to encourage. Engage the courage to speak out in the voice of courage and invite others to do the same.

THE NAAMAN PROTOCOL

Once a person wants to develop the voice of courage, or at least decides to seek his or her dreams in life, the first question that arises is how this can be accomplished. How can Johnny or Mary actually achieve their dream? What can they do to make their goal a reality? How can you do this as well?

The answer, as Lisa and I learned over the years, is to apply the twenty principles listed above.

This brings us to what could be called the Naaman Protocol. A protocol is a guideline of how to do things in the right order and the right way, so you get the results you're looking for. For example, in mechanical work some vehicles require you to remove the gas tank in order to fix a fuel pump. That's the protocol. But if you follow this procedure on all cars, assuming they're all the same, you'll cause a lot of problems—some vehicles have a totally different protocol because to get at the fuel pump you leave the tank in but have to remove the back seat! If you don't know this, you'll create a lot of very costly problems and more work at the very time you're supposed to be fixing things.

In terms of success, knowing the protocol is vital. But few people understand what it is. That's why I wrote this book. The twenty principles are essential, and together they form a protocol of how to put the voice of courage in charge in your life.

Put simply, successful people do a few simple but very difficult things. And they do them consistently. These things include the twenty principles in this book.

> **Put simply, successful people do a few simple but very difficult things. And they do them consistently.**

In the Bible, Naaman, the commander of the army of Syria, approaches the prophet Elisha seeking healing from leprosy. Elisha tells him to do something very simple, bathe himself seven times in the river Jordan. Of course, from a logical standpoint, this makes no sense. Naaman has already bathed many times, and in much cleaner water than that found in the Jordan.

In fact, Naaman almost doesn't do what Elisha recommended. He considers it too simple, and a bit ridiculous. "How could it possibly work?" you can imagine him saying.

But, ultimately, he does what Elisha told him to do. He follows the protocol. The result? He was healed from one of the most dreaded and incurable diseases of his era.

The Naaman Protocol is the act of doing something very simple that brings about great results, even though when you do it you probably can't figure out logically why it will do much good, or even work at all, and even though most people laugh at the idea and tell you it can never succeed. The twenty principles in this book fit that description. They are a lot more difficult than bathing in a river, to be sure, but they are simple. If you do them, if you master them and turn them into habits, and live them, you'll achieve great things.

They are truly powerful.

THE MOST IMPORTANT THING

Indeed, here's the most surprising thing about success, in my experience. I've heard many top leaders and very successful people say the same thing. The hardest part of success is truly controlling our thoughts. Without this skill, without turning this into a habit, no real or lasting success is possible.

> **Successful people do a few simple but very difficult things. And they do them consistently.**

This separates the 1 from the 300, the "10 percent" from the "90".

Successful people know this, often as a result of hard personal experience. Success often takes more than this, to be sure, but without effectively controlling our thoughts we simply will not succeed. The twenty principles are that important.

If you only get one thing out of this book, this is the key point:

**Learn to control your thoughts,
and always ensure that
the voice of courage runs your life.**

The twenty principles make this more simple, more manageable, than just striking out on your own and trying to always keep your thoughts in line. But however you do it, keeping the voice of courage always present and dominant in your mind is an essential part of success.

Doing this is no cakewalk, as I've already said. This is the real battle. Win this, every day, and you'll live your dreams. This is the pitch every one of us simply must hit. Yes, we need to *swing* at it—to try very hard to replace every thought from a self-defeating voice with the voice of courage. But in this case, just swinging isn't enough. We have to actually do this.

It's also the most powerful force you have inside you. The voice of courage is you. Let it speak. Listen to it. Make it the dominant voice in your mind. Never stop doing this. Win this battle and you'll be on the path to living your dreams. Hit this pitch and the grand slam is certain.

I know. I've lived this. In fact, I've lived it both ways: so controlled by self-defeating voices that I couldn't even *swing* the bat, compared to fully engaged with the voice of courage. Having experienced both paths, I promise you the voice of courage is better. Apply these twenty principles. Live them. Embrace them.

They'll change your life.

In short, I invite you to live your dream. Champions have the courage to persist and finish what they start. They also have the courage to start, to begin. The path of success is far from easy, but it is so worth it. And it all hinges on letting the voice of courage run your life.

I've been replacing the voices of self-defeat with the voice of courage now for many years, and I'm going to keep doing it. I'll stop only when I die. Not before.

I invite you to do the same.

Don't hold back. Don't let the wrong voices block your path. If you listen to the same old voices, you'll get the same old results. To get the results you truly want, listen to the voice of courage—make it your dominant voice. Live the life you were meant to live. This is what successful people do. This is the protocol that works.

You know what to do. Twenty things to do, in fact.

Whatever else is going on in your life, embracing the voice of courage inside you will bless you in so many ways. Don't let fear or any other self-defeating voice slow you down or stop you any more. Your dreams are waiting.

So smile. It's time. You're ready.

Stand tall.

Swing!

NOTES

1. Dan Waldschmidt, *EDGY Conversations*, 2014, p. 130

2. See Blake Boles, *Better than College,* 2012, pp. 35-36, and Mary Pilon, "What's a Degree Really Worth?" *Wall Street Journal,* February 2, 2010

3. See David A. Kessler, "Captives of the Mind," *Psychology Today*, May/June 2016, pp. 78-88

4. Ibid.

5. www.recode.net/2016/6/27/12041028/tv-hours-per-week-nielsen

6. As Robert Putnam pointed out in his book *Bowling Alone*, today we tend to engage many of these sports alone rather than in teams, leagues and other community organizations—probably a symptom of the digital age.

7. Between 1850 and 1900 the U.S. divorce rate grew from 3 to 7 percent, by the 1940s this had increased to around 35 percent, and the rate "rose steadily during the 60s, 70s, and 80s," hovering above 50 percent in the 1980s. See divorce.lovetoknow.com/historical_divorce _rate_statistics. Divorce rates have gone down a bit since a high in 1992, which leads some people to believe that the statistics are improving. But the timing

corresponds with fewer people getting married and instead choosing other ways to partner such as civil unions, domestic partnerships, having children together but living separate lives, and cohabitation. In 2015 (the latest available statistics) the rate of people choosing to get married hit an all-time low—and the trend has been heading downward for many years. It will likely continue. Clear statistics on all partners (both married and unmarried) with children breaking up are unavailable or murky. In any case, the rate of divorce and also breakups of partners with children remains far too high.

8. Name and distinguishing details of the story have been changed.

9. English-Ingles.com, "Etymology of Soul"

10. Online Etymology Dictionary, "courage", "core"

11. Some cultures even use the word "spirits" to describe alcohol, which can bring a counterfeit or transient courage, as in "liquid courage." It doesn't last to be sure, but this further illustrates how people have long known that the soul or spirit is the true voice of courage.

12. See op cit., Waldschmidt

13. See the National Endowment for Financial Education, cited in www. cleavland.com/business/index.ssf/why_do_70_percent_of_lottery_w. html, see also "Why So Many Lottery Winner

ACKNOWLEDGMENTS

Over the years I have learned so much from so many. One of the biggest lessons I have learned during this last year is how much hard work and effort goes into the creation of a book—not only the author that pours their heart and soul into the work, but the number of people who either directly or indirectly help accomplish the goal.

I am so grateful for the significant effort put forth by Oliver DeMille. Without his help this would have been just another book. I believe his contribution made this book, my story, come alive in a way that will help the reader apply the principles of courage.

Also, thank you to Orrin and Laurie Woodward who have loved, encouraged and mentored me through so many things, and have given me the belief that I could succeed.

I would be remiss if I did not mention all of the great people at Obstaclés Press. Their hard work and dedication show through from cover to cover of this book.

Most of all I would like to thank my wife Lisa for always believing in me. Without Lisa there is truly no Dan. She has always been by my side, being strong where I was weak, and edifying my strengths. She is truly a living example of what it means to complete her husband. Also, I thank my five daughters, Madison, Jayden, Brooklyn, Bentley and Riley for giving me the inspiration to be a better man and to provide an example of what they will someday look for in a husband.

I am eternally grateful to my Lord and Savior Jesus Christ for His sacrifice and example. It is through His death that we may live and do His work on earth.

Lastly, thank you to the reader for having the courage to change, without waiting for others to change or to act. Instead, you have chosen to lead out front, listening to the voice of courage. You have already shown that you have the hunger to win.

Now: **Take your Swing**.